⊙ Cultural China Series

Liu Tong

CHINESE TEA

A Cultural History and Drinking Guide

Translated by Yue Liwen

CHINA
INTERCONTINENTAL
PRESS

图书在版编目（CIP）数据

中国茶：英文/ 刘彤编著；乐利文译.－2版.－北京：五洲传播出版社，2010.1
ISBN 978－7－5085－1667－7

Ⅰ.中 …　Ⅱ.刘…　Ⅲ.茶－文化－中国－英文　Ⅳ.TS971
中国版本图书馆CIP数据核字（2009）第180880号

CHINESE TEA
A Cultural History and Drinking Guide

Author: Liu Tong

Translator: Yue Liwen

Polisher: Chen Bingmiao

Executive Editor: Zhang Hong

Art Director: Tang Ni

Photo Credit: Li Yuxiang

Publisher: China Intercontinental Press (6 Beixiaomachang, Lianhuachi Donglu, Haidian District, Beijing 100038, China)

Tel: 86-10-58891281

Website: www.cicc.org.cn

Printer: C&C Joint Printing Co., (Beijing) Ltd.

Edition: Jan. 2010, 2nd edition, 3rd print run

Format: 155×230mm   1/16

Price: RMB 96.00 (*yuan*)

Contents

Preface

Tea is a friend of meditation, keeping the heart immerged in profound tranquility. Tea is wings of imagination, lifting people above the mundane world while remaining clear minded, getting people nearer wisdom rather than losing sanity. Therefore in nearly every Eastern country people have the same habit of drinking tea, because people in the east need this simple but not insipid drink. This is a tradition of life as well as of culture, just like the Eastern wisdom that they admire, which is featured in the spirit of self-reflection.

Because of their different producing techniques, Chinese tea is divided into six major types—green tea, black tea, oolong tea, dark tea, yellow tea and white tea. Some people say that green tea, simple and light, stands for the scholasticity of south China; black tea, mild and reserved, is quite ladylike; oolong tea, warm and persistent, resembles the perseverance of gymnosophists; dark tea, with lingering aftertaste, symbolizes the wisdom of the elderly, and so on and so forth.

China is the homeland of tea, taking a leading position in the planting, producing and drinking of tea. The discovery and usage of tea has had a history of four or five thousand years in China. From the earliest fresh-boiled tea taken as a kind of soup to later dried-and-preserved tea, from the simple green tea to the blooming of six major kinds of tea, tea, which started catching on in the Tang (618–906) and Song (960–1279) dynasties, has carried itself to the contemporary times. The flavor of tea, which is sometimes thin and sometimes thick, seemingly bitter but actually sweet, has flown throughout the long history from ancient times up to now. What is more, with its unique appeal, tea has broken the bound of fields and been brought to all parts of the world.

The origin of tea is lost among history and legends. What can be roughly confirmed is that tea originated in the southwest of China. In Yunnan and other places there still exist wild tea trees over 1,000 years old. It is said that the first man to discover what tea can do is Shen Nong—the father of agriculture and herbal medicine in China. In time immemorial, people knew very little about plants. In order to find out which plants could be eaten and which couldn't, Shen Nong tasted various kinds of plants to find out their features as food or medicine. Fortunately, Shen Nong had a transparent stomach, which made it possible for him, after he had eaten the plants, to observe the reactions in his stomach caused by them. That is where the famous story of "Shen Nong Tasting A Hundred Plants" came from. One day, after walking for a long time, Shen Nong felt tired and thirsty, so he rested under a tree and started a fire to boil water. Suddenly some tree leaves fell into the water hollowware on the fire. Shen Nong drank the water and found it not only sweet and tasteful, but freshening as well. He found his exhaustion all gone, so he finished all the water in the hollowware. Another tale is a little different from this one, but more amazing. It is said that Shen Nong tried 72 different kinds of poisonous plants in a day and he lay on the ground, barely alive. At this moment, he noticed several leaves dropping from the tree beside him, giving off gusts of fragrance. What with curiosity and with habit, Shen Nong put the leaves in his mouth and chewed them. After a little while, he felt well and energetic again. So he picked more leaves to eat and thus cleared all the poison in his body. Whatever way the story goes, tea interested Shen Nong and attracted him to do further research on its characteristics. The ancient Chinese medical book called *Shen Nong Herbal*, which is attributed to Shen Nong, says that "tea tastes bitter. Drinking it, one can think quicker, sleep less, move lighter, and see clearer." That is the earliest book to put down the medical functions of tea.

When it came to the Zhou Dynasty (1046–256 BC), the function of tea to freshen one's body and clear one's mind gradually replaced its function as medicine. People started drying tea leaves to better preserve it. When they made tea, they put the leaves into the hollowware and made a kind of thick soup. The princes of the Zhou Dynasty were used to this thick soup, but due to its bitterness, it didn't catch on.

In the Han Dynasty (206 BC–AD 220), both the collecting and processing of wild tea leaves were improved. Tea became a tasteful drink and was fancied by the nobles, and it became very popular among them. In the time of Wei (220–265) and Jin (265–420), when metaphysics came into fashion and people got interested in talking, tea, in place of wine, has became the drink of banquet. People preferred tea's freshness and purity to wine's violence and intoxication. The last emperor of the Three-Kingdom time (220–280) is Sun Hao (reign from 264–280). He asked his ministers to drink six liters of wine every time he held a banquet. One minister was not good at drinking, so he secretly asked Sun if he could drink tea instead. In fact the relationship between tea and wine has always been subtle. Wine drinking needs a hilarious environment while tea drinking prefers quietness. They are different in many aspects, but they are also the best partners because tea can quench one's drunkenness. In later times, this unity of opposites between tea and wine was reflected in a dialogue between them in a book called On Tea and Wine.

It can be seen that to this time, tea has been spread from the kingdom of Shu (221–263) to the lower reaches of Yangtze River. In the time of Eastern and Western Jins and Northern and Southern dynasties (265–589), rulers advocated drinking tea and eating simple food in order to restrain the competition in extravagance among nobles. Buddhism and Taoism played an indispensable role in the spreading of tea. Buddhists liked tea because it prevented people from dreariness and languor, while Taoists believed that tea helped people stay young and become immortal. At that time people began making tea cakes from tea leaves. When they wanted to make tea, they ground the cakes into powder and put it, along with other condiments, into hot water.

It is said in history that "tea started in the Tang Dynasty and flourished in the Song Dynasty." People in the Tang Dynasty invented a method called "Steaming Green" to get rid of the flavor of grass from tea leaves. They picked tea leaves, ground them after steaming, made them into cakes, dried them and then sealed them up for keeping. There were many ways to call tea before Tang. One of them was 荼, a Chinese character meaning bitter. Tang people crossed off one stroke and changed it into 茶. This character has many interesting connotations in its shape. Its bottom is 木, meaning wood; the top is 艹, meaning grass; between them is 人, meaning people. This suggests the harmony between human being and nature. It was also in Tang that teahouse in its real sense came into being. In some big cities were tea shops. They made tea for their customers and the tea leaves in their shops were mountainous. Poems and articles dedicated to tea also appeared. A large group of poets like Lu Tong and Bai Juyi all wrote about tea. Furthermore, Tang possessed the first definitive commentary on tea—*The Book of Tea*, which was the first of its kind in China and in the world as well. The book, which contained a comprehensive summary of all aspects of the culture of tea, including medical function, picking, making, cooking, utensil, etc., was then a complete expression of knowledge on tea. Its autho—Lu Yu (733–c.804) was consequently called "Saint of Tea" by later generations. During this period, tea became the most popular commodity in foreign trade. Japanese Buddhists in China brought tea leaves back to Japan. For the sake of easier transportation, tea leaves were made into bricks. People broke a little piece when they wanted to drink tea.

The Song Dynasty was a golden age for tea. The business of teahouse was even more blooming. The calligrapher Cai Xiang

(1012–1067)wrote *Record of Tea* and Emperor Huizong—Zhao Ji (1082–1135) wrote *General Remarks on Tea*. When the Ming Dynasty (1368–1644) succeeded, the tea culture, which was once damaged by the Mongolians, underwent a renaissance. The familiar dark tea, green tea, and oolong tea were all developed during this time. Zhu Yuanzhang (reign 1368–1398), the first emperor of Ming, changed roll tea to loose tea, and the tradition has been kept ever since.

With the ever better understanding of tea, people were no longer contented with picking wild tea leaves, but opened tea gardens and planted tea trees. Processing of tea was also getting mature. Furthermore, due to the different processing methods, there appeared six major types of tea. Nor did people continue to take tea as food or medicine. Drinking tea became a spiritual need, containing deep cultural meanings. The tea ceremony in China consists of not only the choice of tea, but many other elements such as water, utensil, time, occasion, etc. There are also detailed requirements for the drinkers. Meanwhile, in the process of the popularization of tea, people in different regions and of different nationalities have developed their unique custom of tea drinking. Guangdong people like drinking morning tea, Fujian people prefer Kongfu tea, Hunan has Lei tea, Sichuan people love covered-bowl tea, people of Bai nationality treat guests with "Three-Course Tea," Tibetan people prefer buttered tea and Inner-Mongolian people like milk tea... The various tea customs constitute the rich and profound Chinese tea culture.

The wonderful tea leaves were spread to all parts of the world through intercourse among nations. Japanese Monks took tea seeds, techniques of tea making, and tea utensils back to Japan, which led to the appearance of Japanese tea ceremony. The earliest record of tea in Europe was in the travel notes of an Arab. Marco Polo mentioned in his notes that a Chinese minister of financee was deposed because he excessively levied taxes on tea. At the end of the 16th century, the Dutch brought such a message to Europe that there was a kind of magic leaves in the east, from which tasty drinks could be made. That was the first time that the Europeans heard of tea. In 1610, East India Company was the first to sell tea to Europe, after which the habit of drinking tea took root there. In 1636, tea entered France and two years later, it entered Russia, whereas the big tea-consuming Britain didn't have tea until 1650.

Currently over 450 chemical substances have been discovered in tea, some of which are microelements capable of supplementing nutrient substances needed by human body and some other can prevent or cure diseases. Green tea is a nutritious drink full of vitamins. It contains a kind of hydroxybenzene, which can restrain cancer cell and thus prevent or resist cancer. Oolong tea can control the absorption of dextrose by human body, and can help lose weight. Black tea is mild, which is good for phlegm reducing, digesting, and arousing appetite, especially good for people with weak spleen and stomach. Pu'er tea can prevent cardiovascular diseases, and has been internationally known as "Tea of Longevity" for a long time. Tea leaves are also helpful in radiation prevention, which is especially suitable for people who have constant contact with computers.

Coming to the 21st century, tea is no longer confined as drinks. The essence of tea is often found in shampoo, toothpaste, and other daily necessities. Health care products like ointment also contain tea. The story of tea is far from over.

Good Tea from Remote Mountain

Trees were growing in the mountainous and rainy primitive forests in Yunnan, Guizhou, Sichuan and other Provinces in the very beginning. Later they were planted and transplanted by people, who gradually summarized that tea trees liked places where were warm, damp and in the shade. Generally speaking, the best temperature for them is between 18°C and 25°C. They stop growing when it's below 5°C and are likely to die when it's over 40°C. Tea trees like to grow in damp places and are very demanding about the water content in air and soil. Tea trees are easily influenced by height. Take the famous Wuyi Rock tea for example, Zheng Rock tea from the top of Wuyi Mountain, Ping Rock tea from the middle of the mountain, and Zhou tea from the valley are differently graded—the higher, the more valuable. Besides, sunshine and soil also play a decisive role in the growth of tea trees.

Sanqing tea bowl of Qing Dynasty.

Ancient people thought that tea trees are not regarded as high or low because of their breeds. The differences come from their growing conditions. Regions with advantaged environment can more often produce rare types of tea. That's why it is said that "famous mountains give birth to famous tea." Taking for instance the Chinese famous mountains that are listed as "World's Inheritance," we have Rock tea from Wuyi Mountain, Maofeng from Mount Huangshan, Cloud-and-Fog from Mount Lushan, Maofeng from Mount Emei, Maojian from Wuling Mountain, Snow-Bud from Mount Qingcheng, and many other traditional famous teas. This shows how important it is for keeping tea trees' vitality to have high forest coverage rate, rich fauna and flora, and healthy ecological environment.

< The real taste of tea can be felt better when drinking it with a feeling of tasting life. Provided by Huang Rui.

Picking, choosing, and baking tea leaves. Photo by Li Yuxiang.

Lu Yu said in his The Book of Tea, "Tea is good wood in the south." "Good wood" is a eulogy referring to the characteristics of tea trees. Lu Yu used a series of metaphors to describe tea trees, "Tea… its tree looks like melon reed, leaves are like Gardenia's, flowers are like white rosebushes, fruit is like palm's, stem is like clove's, and root looks like walnut's." Tea trees are generally divided into three types-shrub, arbor, and minor arbor. The shrub type stands 3 to 5 meters high in natural conditions. Wild tea trees can even reach 10 meters high. The arbor type is usually only 1.5 to 3 meters. Cultivated tea trees are short because they are pruned.

The children in tea-planting area usually take some vacation to help picking up tea. Photo by Li Yuxiang.

Tea trees originally grow in the wild, later they are cultivated by humans. Limited by natural conditions, tea areas in China are mainly in the south. But with the improvement of cultivating skills, these areas tend to spread continuously. In the Tang Dynasty there were 8 main tea-producing areas in China. In the Song Dynasty, these areas were everywhere in the south of Qinling Mountains and Huai River. The Ming Dynasty basically settled the distribution pattern of tea areas today.

For a very long time people thought wild tea leaves were more precious. The Book of Tea said that "those in the wild are superior while those in the garden are inferior." In the Tang Dynasty, people in every tea area chose the best leaves to pay tribute to the royalties. Those were called "Tribute Tea." The most celebrated tribute tea at that time was the Purple Bamboo Shoot Tea, growing near Mount Guzhu in Huzhou, Zhejiang Province. In order to satisfy the royalties' request for wild Purple Bamboo Shoot Tea, the local people made great efforts. An official who superintended the

Going to pick up tea leaves. Photo by Li Yuxiang.

production of tribute tea wrote in a poem that the leave pickers had to climb high cliffs to pick leaves, but they could only get a handful in a whole morning. Tang Dynasty had a large demand for tribute tea, the largest amount being 9200 kilos. Wild tea trees could not meet such a huge demand, so part of the tribute tea were produced from tea gardens cultivated by men, but those were less good in quality.

The cultivation of tea trees has a long history. Wild tea trees, after long years of human cultivation, have changed a lot in their appearances. Gradually they were mainly short shrubs, and their growing environment was not confined to mountains only. Tang people already had a very deep understanding of the growth characteristics of tea. In accordance with tea's preference for shade, Tang people planted tea in the shaded north side or under mulberries. Tea trees usually lived in wet and rainy regions, but too much rain might spoil the roots, so tea planting set a high standard for soil. According to Lu Yu, the soil in which tea trees lived not only needed a good drainage, but had to contain a little acid. Based on this, Tang people invented the way of digging deep channels and ridges at either side of the tree, so as to vent the unwanted water in time, thus preventing the root from soaking in water too long, which could lead to the death of the tree. At that time, tea trees were seeded and rarely replanted. People believed that planting tea was like planting melon. It required 3 years of cultivation before it could be picked. Lu Yu divided the entire country into 8 major tea producing areas. Residents within those areas mostly undertook the planting or producing of tea leaves. In some places 60-70% of the residents lived by tea. The planting, making, and selling of tea became economic lifelines of these areas.

The Song Dynasty witnessed the height of splendor of tea, and tea cultivation made greater progress. In Emperor Huizong's *General Remarks on Tea*, he used the theory of mutual complementation of *Yin* and *Yang* to perfect the planting of tea trees. He said that on the hillside, trees should be planted in the sunny side while they should be in the shade side of the garden. That's because hill soil belonged to *Yin*, and tea leaves from there were thin in taste, needing sunshine to neutralize them. Garden soil was too fertile and made the leaves strong, so they had to avoid direct sunshine. People in the Song Dynasty paid more attention to the air permeability of soil. They added chaff and burned clay to soil to ameliorate the soil fabric. Every June garden workers would scarify the soil and earth up for the tea trees, and would weed on the hottest noon in summer. They pulled the weeds out with roots and insolated them under the sun, and the dried weeds were to be used as fertilizers for the trees. This method combined scarification, weeding, and fertilization, effectively saving manpower and materials. It could be called "killing three birds with one stone." Unlike Tang people's planting tea trees under mulberries, Song people took tung oil trees to be the best partner for tea trees, because tung trees were tall while tea trees were short, and they could bring out the best of each other. What's more, tea trees disliked heat in summer and couldn't stand coldness in winter. Tung trees gave out broad and big leaves in early spring, so they could provide tea trees with shade. In autumn, tung leaves fell early, which made it easy for sunlight to shine directly upon the tea trees to give them enough warmth.

In the Ming Dynasty, more theoretical remarks were made upon the cultivation of tea leaves. Ming people believed that tea leaves grown in the plain absorbed the flavor of soil, while those on the cliff could absorb the marrow of sunshine, breeze, rain and dew; therefore mountains were the best locations for tea planting. During this time, vegetative propagation was invented. Branches were cut off tea trees to be replanted elsewhere. After many years of growing, tea trees no longer gave birth to new shoots because the soil got lean. That's the time to get rid of the old branches by chopping or burning the old trees. After that new shoots would pop out from the roots in the following spring.

Tea picking normally take place in spring, summer and autumn,

Autumn is just the picking-up season for oolong tea of Wuyi Mountain.

and the leaves picked in each season are accordingly called spring tea, summer tea and autumn tea, which are different in their shape and quality. Spring tea should be picked around Waking of Insects (near March 6th) and Grain Rain (near April 20th). If earlier, leaves haven't matured, while if later, they are old and have stem, neither is good. Spring tea picked from Waking of Insects till Pure Brightness (April 5th) are what we call Pre-Brightness tea or First tea. They take on a light verdant color and taste pure with a little acerbity. Two weeks after Pure Brightness is Grain Rain, when fine rain descends in south China and brings nutrition to all kinds of crops. That is the second high time for picking spring tea. Leaves picked after Pure Brightness and before Grain Rain are called Pre-Rain tea, and those picked after that time are called After-Rain tea. The price of spring tea differs according to their picking time. Generally speaking, green tea in early spring is deemed as the best in quality. Leaves picked in the current year are called new tea while those put away for over a year are called old tea. Green tea and oolong tea are better to be new while Pu'er tea tastes better and costs more after longer years.

Lu Yu prescribed that tea picking should be done in right weather. Leaves shouldn't be picked in cloudy days if there was rain, nor in sunny days if there were clouds. Later generations amended and developed this regulation. Generally speaking, tea picking should be done around the Waking of Insects (the 3rd solar term) and Grain Rain (the 4th solar term). Before that tea leaves hadn't completed growth and after that leaves were old and had peduncles—neither was good. Garden tea leaf picking in the plain should be carried out before the sun was up, for once the sun rose, its strong light would wither the leaves and made them lose water. If so, the leaves after processing would taste much worse. In the mountain there was much fog, so tea should be picked after the sun rose and fog dispersed. Some reckon that tea leaves picked at this time could stop coughing, dispel phlegm, and cure many other illnesses. Tea leaves should be picked with clean finger tips rather than fingers, as fingers might be stained with dust and sweat to taint the leaves. The picked leaves would be sorted into different grades. Different grades couldn't be mixed together.

Leaves of tea trees are the major material in tea making, and are therefore the most important. The fresher the leaves are, the more delicious they taste after processing, so leaves are normally picked when they are still little shoots. The top shoots and young shoots in the tip of a new branch are both covered with soft hairs in the shaded side, which is a sign of delicacy and high quality. On the same branch, the soft hairs are mostly on the shoots, dense and long. Next to shoots are young leaves, and then tender leaves. As the leaves mature, hairs become shorter and then drop off. These leaves can only make low-quality products, or cannot be used at all.

The Art of Tea-making

Picking up the famous tea Pilochun. Photo by Li Yuxiang.

Chinese people generally drink tea in two major ways. Some, according to their personal taste, like to add salt, sugar, milk, shallot, orange peel, mint, longan, and Chinese date into tea while drinking, whereas some others only cook tea with boiled water without adding anything to spoil the original taste of tea. This is called "pure drinking," in which way some people drink with big bowls to satisfy thirst, and some others who emphasize the color, fragrance and taste of tea and are particular about the water quality would sip and appreciate the tea slowly. If equal importance is given to the drinking atmosphere, tea cooking technique, as well as public relations, one has to go to tea houses to appreciate "tea ceremony." Tea ceremonies are not mystic. They are both commonplace and elevated, just like the character of Chinese people, casual and natural, not restricted by certain patterns.

The Chinese have an inveterate habit of drinking tea. The way of drinking tea goes through a change from simplicity to complication and then back to simplicity again—from frying to cooking, from roll tea to loose tea. At the very beginning, people put leaves directly into the pot to boil, just as Shen Nong did. Later, with the improvement of tea production and preservation skills, people ground tea leaves to make tea cake and added water when drinking it. Up to Ming Dynasty, loose tea leaves completely replaced tea cake to take the lead in tea drinking, and has continued ever since.

It's recorded in documents that as early as 2000 BC, Sichuan Province in southwest China already produced tea leaves, and even presented them as tribute to the royal family of Kingdom Zhou. Some

Tea as a Food Ingredient
Tea is not only a drink but also a food ingredient. In the southwest of China, people to this day continue to use tea as a food in everyday life. Maybe they mix tea leaves with oil and salt or ginger and salt or with sesame seeds and beans, or else they stir-fry it with garlic to make a dish to be eaten with rice; another possibility is to pickle new tea-leaves and eat them as a side dish. In the east of China, where green tea abounds, there are quite a number of famous high-grade banquet dishes which are made with tea leaves or brewed tea.

The painting *Cooking Tea* by Ding Yunpeng of Ming Dynasty.

scholars also found out that the discovery and usage of tea has a history of at least 10,000 years. Still, it has been a long time before tea was widely accepted as a kind of drink. Within a very long period, tea is as important as medicine, or even more important than, it is food and drink.

The earliest way of making use of tea is probably that people picked leaves off the tree and put them directly in mouth, just like what Shen Nong did. According to the record in ancient books of China, in the time of Spring and Autumn (770–476 BC), a chancellor named Yan Yin (?–500 BC) led a very frugal life. He ate rice and few meat dishes every day, with some Ming (meaning tea in Chinese) dishes. What is Ming dish? It is fresh tea leaves used as a dish to accompany rice. This custom of eating tea as a dish is still in action in some ethnic groups of China nowadays. Some ethnic groups in Yunnan pound tea leaves into little pieces, add garlic, pepper and salt, and make delicious cold dishes of them. Tea leaves can also be pickled in bamboo canisters. Knead the fresh leaves after steaming them soft, put them in a bamboo canister and pestle them tight, dry them, and seal the canister for the leave pieces to ferment. After two or three months, the pieces are taken out, put in a jar, and added spices suck as balm. You can take them out any time you want to eat. Even in the time of Wei and Jin, and Northern and Southern dynasties, when drinking tea was in full swing because of the influence of Buddhism, the custom of having tea as a dish was not entirely extinct. At that time, some boiled tea with porridge, called Ming porridge. Some others boiled tea with flour, called flour tea. Today, whenever you enter a chop house in any city in China, you can almost always order tea eggs. Add tea leaves when boiling eggs, so the eggs will have the fragrance of tea leaves–this is an old tradition of China.

In the time of Wei, Jin and Northern and Southern dynasties, it was popular to grind tea leaves and make them into tea cakes. The main processing method was "steaming green" to take out the grass flavor by steaming. It included steaming, drenching,

The method of "frying green" for the tea Pilochun. Photo by Li Yuxiang.

pressing, grinding, baking, and many other procedures. After picking and sorting the leaves, people washed them several times to scour off the dust and impurities. After being steamed in a hollowware, the leaves were drenched with cold water to cool. After that the water should be pressed out and leaves were put into certain containers for grinding. The ground leaves were made into the shape of cakes with holes in the middle for thread to string them together. These cakes were then put into a sealed room to bake and dry, after which cakes could be sealed up for keeping. When drinking the tea, the cakes were crumbled and shallot, ginger, orange and other condiments could be added.

Lu Yu's *The Book of Tea* made stipulations as to the drinking utensils, the choice of water, and elaborately introduced the drinking method of "Three Boil," which is as follows. First, bake the tea cake on fire a little while to get rid of the water in the cakes and to render the tea cakes hard and crisp. Then grind the cakes into powder with specially made tools. What follows is to fry tea, for which an ancient cooking vessel called *Ding* (a huge pot on three posts) or *Fu* (like a kettle) is used. Lu Yu thought that salt could add to the fresh flavor of tea, so he maintained that salt should be added when water just started boiling. When the water boils for the second time, scoop it out with a gourd ladle and stir the water with bamboo clips to even the temperature. After fully stirring the water, drop tea powder into it and go on stirring. When froth appears, pour the ladle of water just now out for tea to cool and for more froth. It is at this moment that *Ding* or *Fu* can be removed from the fire and tea can be drunk. It is also stated in the book that three bowls of tea would be enough if the tea is top class, five bowls for tea of a little less good quality. If there are guests, three

Tea Competitions
The old Chinese custom of holding tea competitions started in the Five Dynasties period (907 to 959), when a writer of lyrics, He Ningguan, a high official who was very fond of tea, set up a 'Brew Society'. Colleagues in public office invited each other to drink tea instead of to dinner, and they amused themselves with tea competitions. By the Tang and Song period the competitions came to serve the purpose of picking out the best teas to be tribute teas for the court to use. The competitions also became more serious, with special classes for colour, flavour and leaf shape, leading to a comprehensive evaluation and comparison of the teas in all their aspects. The Song dynasty also for this reason produced a number of leading tea connoisseurs, and poets and painters were induced to try and capture the atmosphere of tea competitions in their poems and paintings.

bowls are drunk by each when there are five guests and five bowls are drunk by each if there are seven guests. After all, tea is not a drink that is the more the better. The amount of tea you drink has something to do with decorum as well as its taste.

It can be said that it was after Lu Yu wrote *The Book of Tea* that, under the leadership of scholars, people elevated the state of tea from eating, drinking to appreciating. It has become a high-taste delight of life to appreciate tea, which gave people unworldly spiritual joy. On the other hand, it also showed that the state of "plain tea and simple food" could no longer meet some one's requirements, and developing and summarizing tea techniques opened a new field for them to seek a better and more refined life style.

When it came to Song Dynasty, the pursuit for refinement of tea drinking reached its peak and became a ceremonial activity. Song Dynasty inherited the usage of tea cakes but abandoned the method of frying for cooking. There are a lot of preparations before cooking. First the tea cakes should be checked. If preserved for years, the cakes should be soaked in boiling water for a while to dispel about one Liang of grease. If it's a cake of the same year, it can be ground into powder directly. Song people chose narrow necked bottle to boil water and the water was better to be boiled just twice. Before cooking, the tea cups should be warmed with slow fire for fear that the boiling water poured into the cup would quickly cool down. Then put the ground tea powder into the cup and add little boiling water to mix them into the shape of cream. Then slowly add more water and keep stirring it with a little brushing broom to create froth. Song people liked the original taste of tea leaves and sneered at people's adding salt, ginger or other condiments into tea. The ceremony of tea drinking reached its height in Song Dynasty. Men of literature and writing not only held tea parties frequently, but competed in their skill at cooking tea in those parties. These were called "Contest of Tea" or "Competition of Ming," which were in vogue for quite a while.

The method of "sunning green" for the tea Longjing. Photo by Li Yuxiang.

During Tang and Song, the tribute tea exclusive for royal use was all cake tea, and tea cakes in Song were especially delicate. After the leaves were steamed and dried, they were ground with water and adjusted into glue, only then were they put into moulds to be molded into shape. Roll tea or cake tea made in this way was of various shapes-square, round, oval, polygon, etc. There were various vivid patterns on the surface as well. After the molding, cakes had to be baked from 6 to 15 times before they were drenched with hot water to make their color fresh and bright. Finally, the drenched cakes were put into a sealed room to be fanned to cool rapidly. The next day they should be baked and dried with slow fire. Only after all these steps was the beautiful and wonderful cake tea at last completed.

The tribute tea in Song was mostly in the pattern of dragon and phoenix, called Dragon & Phoenix Cake. Each tribute tea could only be presented for 5 years. After 5 years new types should be developed, so local officers in charge of the collecting of tea always racked their brains to design something new. Cai Xiang, writer of Record of Tea, succeeded in inventing the more delicate small-dragon cake, based on the original big-dragon cake. 20 small-dragon cakes weighed about 0.5 kilo, worth as much as 1/10 kilo of gold. Afterwards, a man named Jia Qing invented Miyun Dragon tea. Since every step in the making process was made as perfect as possible, this new kind of tea cake was greatly favored by the king for its refinement and delicacy. It even brought the king some troubles. Miyun Dragon tea was produced in a small amount. After sacrificed to the ancestors and enjoyed by the king of Song, there wasn't much left. However, it was

A tea pot of Tang Dynasty with a handle and colorful patterns.

< Tea utensils. Photo by Zheng Ligang, provided by *China Tourism*, Hong Kong.

so exquisite and renowned that royal relatives and close ministers always asked the king for some. The king was very annoyed by the constant importuning, so he gave orders to stop the production of this tea. After this, Miyun Dragon tea was even more expensive.

In spite of its easy preservation, tea cake is time and energy consuming when being made, and inconvenient when being drunk, so it was less and less welcomed. What is more, leaves will lose part of their juice in the process of being made into cakes and are easy to produce grease, which is hardly acceptable for the tea lovers who attach much importance to the tranquility and natural charm of tea. Therefore, after Yuan Dynasty, the natural taste of tea was getting more and more attention. Taking over the regime from Yuan, the first emperor of Ming Dynasty, Zhu Yuanzhang, abolished the complicated and costly cake tea and accepted only loose tea as tribute, in order to restore the country from the after-war state of ruin. He also advocated cooking tea with full leaves rather than grinding leaves into powder. A man named Lu Shusheng in Ming Dynasty wrote *Book of Jasmine*, in which he specifically pointed out the ways of cooking tea. In summer, boiled water should be poured into the apparatus before leaves were put in for fear the water would burn the leaves to be ripe. In winter, leaves came in before hot water for fear low water temperature couldn't bring out the taste of tea. Accordingly, Ming people changed their tea apparatus from big pot to small pot, because in big pot, tea taste dispersed too quickly, while small pot could better keep its fragrance. In this way, with Zhu Yuanzhang's earnest advocacy, loose tea soon took the position of cake tea. By the middle of Ming Dynasty, the once highly fashionable tea cakes and competitions of Ming already belonged to the past, almost completely out of existence.

Loose tea was not an invention of Ming people because the "frying green" method of making loose tea was recorded as early as in Tang Dynasty, though the technique of "frying green" was perfected in Ming. Frying green was far less complicated than steaming green, but there was still much to pay attention to. First, the tool should not be unused iron pan, which had the smell of iron. Second, the pan should not be tainted with oil, for the flavor of tea was thin and weak and could be easily spoiled by oil. When frying green, the pan should be first warmed with slow fire, and then leaves were put into it. The amount of tea leaves should not be too large at a time, only about 0.5 kilo. When the pan began making cracking sounds and leaves softened, we used quick fire and fried rapidly. Wooden fingertips should be used when frying green, quick stirring and frying made sure that the leaves were evenly heated. Meanwhile fans were used to let out the heat in time. When leaves were done, they were spread thinly on a dustpan, fanned to cool, and softly kneaded and twisted to let the tea oil thoroughly immerge. In the end, twisted leaves were put back into the pan and baked and dried with slow fire.

Heating is a crucial factor in steaming green or frying green. Too big fire ages and withers the leaves while too small fire can't dispel the grass smell and can't fully keep the tea fragrance. Therefore our ancestors set many regulations about fire. For instance, when frying green, it's better to choose branches as fuel rather than dry leaves, for dry leaves burn and go out very quickly, which makes it difficult to control the temperature. In order to better control temperature, some people suggest using charcoal fire, particularly when baking and drying.

It goes in the myths that tea attracted the recognition and advocacy of Shen Nong for its capability to detoxify. May be it's because of this that has long kept Chinese people's favor for its medical value. The famous litterateur Sima Xiangru (179–117 BC) of Western Han has recorded 20 kinds of medicine of Sichuan, tea being one of them. A celebrity in the Southern Dynasty drank a *Dou* (a Chinese measurement unit, about 10 liters) of tea a time, and was jokingly called by people as *"Lou Zhi,"* meaning bottomless cup. Why did he drink so much tea? Contemporary people believed that tea could not only make drunken people sober up and keep people awake, but could remove tiredness and keep people strong and energetic. It could also help people dispel anxiety or irritation, and even elevated them to be celestial. An emperor of Sui Dynasty (581–618) fell ill and a monk told him that tea could cure his disease. The famous doctor of Ming Dynasty Li Shizhen (1518–1593) wrote in his *Compendium of Materia Medica*, "Tea is bitter and cold, the coldest of colds and most able to subdue human heat. Once the heat goes, the body goes right." As a result, for many years, tea is not only a drink, but is also used as a cheap herbal medicine.

Well-known People and Books about Tea

茶者，南方之嘉木也。一尺二尺迺至數十尺。其巴山峽川有兩人合抱者，伐而掇之。其樹如瓜蘆，葉如梔子，花如白薔薇，實如栟櫚，蒂如丁香，根如胡桃。

廣州似茶，苦澀，栟櫚蒲葵之屬，其子似茶，胡桃與茶根皆下孕兆至瓦礫苗木上抽。

其字或從草，或從木，或草木并。從草，當作茶，其字出開元文字；從木，當作搽，其字出

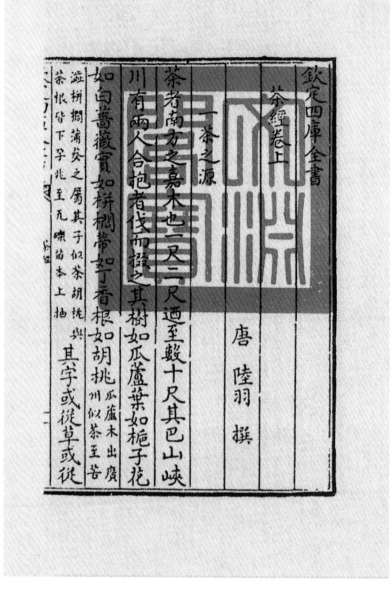

The Book of Tea, compiled into *The Siku Quanshu* (complete *Library of the Four Branches of Literature*) of Qing Dynasty.

Chinese tea culture is of long standing. People not only found out various ways of making, cooking and drinking tea through practice, but also summarized them and put them down in books. After Lu Yu wrote The Book of Tea as an example, commentary about tea appeared in almost every historical time, with numerous articles in this respect. These have been crucial clues for us to trace the historical development of tea.

Lu Yu and *The Book of Tea*

Lu Yu's *The Book of Tea* was the world's first commentary on tea, exerting a profound influence after its appearance. Books on tea in later generations were all affected by it in one way or another. Because of this, Lu Yu was idolized by later generations as "God of Tea," "Saint of Tea," "Ancestor of Tea," "The Immortal of Tea," and so on. There also emerged innumerable stories and legends based on Lu Yu.

Lu Yu belongs to Tang Dynasty, born around AD 733 and died in AD 804. He was an orphan and was adopted by a monk named Zhiji. It is said that one day when Zhiji went out, he found three wile geese protecting a newly born baby with their wings. Surprised at this, Zhiji took the baby back out of compassion. Lu Yu grew up in the temple. Zhiji intended him to become a Buddhist, but knowing that Buddhists couldn't marry nor have offspring, Lu Yu was more inclined to Confucianism. Angry at this, Zhiji punished Lu Yu by making him do all kinds of chores like cleaning, herding, washing toilets, etc. Tea drinking was very popular in temples at that time, so naturally Lu Yu got to know something about tea.

What Counts as Good Tea in the Classic of Tea
The Classic of Tea collects together the main fruits of tea lore up to the Tang dynasty, and is also China's earliest encyclopedia of tea. It goes back to the earliest origins of tea, and after discussing the names for 'tea' throughout history, the different methods of cultivating tea bushes and the varieties of tea and their flavours, goes on to set out certain basic criteria used in the Tang period to tell good tea from bad. At that time tea from wild plants was thought the best, and cultivated teas were considered somewhat inferior; among the wild plants, they prized purple leafed tea from tree-shaded plants on south-facing slopes, and rated green leaves below them; as for leaf shape, curly leaves were best and flat leaves were less good. These standards were not only those of the writer Lu Yu, but also those generally current in his time, and to this day they are still regarded as valid by the people of the rich tea producing area of Wuyi Mountain in Fujian province.

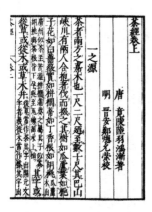

The Book of Tea, *Ming Dynasty.*

The Book of Tea, published in Japan in 1844.

Later, finding the temple too stifling, Lu Yu ran away to join a theatrical troupe at the age of 12. He played puppet show, acrobatics and magic. Talented and versatile, Lu Yu was soon promoted to the position of director. During one show, he was recognized by an official who helped him get a chance to be educated. Afterwards, Lu Yu traveled around and inspected local tea areas, often consulting tea farmers as to how to pick and make tea. With years of accumulation, he withdrew to live in a remote mountain and put his heart into writing his book. Eventually Lu Yu succeeded in accomplishing the grandiose and ever-eminent masterpiece—*The Book of Tea*.

Historical literature doesn't say much as to exactly how fabulous Lu Yu's tea-cooking skill really is, but folklores can make up for this lack. One story has it that once an official met Lu Yu near Yangtze River. Knowing that Lu Yu's tea-cooking skill was the world's best and the water in Nanling area of Yangtze River was of top quality, the official found it a once-in-a-lifetime opportunity and especially sent soldiers to Nanling to fetch water. Before long, a soldier brought the water. Scooping it out and glancing at it briefly, Lu Yu said, "although the water is from Yangtze River, it doesn't belong to Nanling but likely from the coast." The soldier argued, "I went to Nanling in person and hundreds of people saw me draw water there. How can it be wrong?" Lu Yu didn't say anything. The soldier poured water into a pot. When it was half full, Lu Yu suddenly said, "Stop! From here it's Nanling water." The soldier was astonished. The fact was the soldier did draw a full jar of water, but the boat was so unstable that half of the water spilled over. Afraid of being criticized, he refilled the jar with coast water, only to find that Lu Yu exposed his lie at one glance. Both shocked and scared, the soldier exclaimed that God of Tea did deserve his fame and dared not hide the truth longer.

Lu Yu wasn't very good-looking and was innately inarticulate. But he was born with a generous heart, sincerely admiring other people's merits and felt genuinely sad when seeing others' demerits as if he suffered from those too. Because of this, many poets and personages liked to make friends with him. Writing *The Book of Tea*, Lu Yu made quite a sensation, so the emperor called for him to be an official. However, Lu Yu enjoyed a life of freedom and leisure, lingering in tea gardens every day and sang and relaxed with friends. In his old age, Lu Yu changed his hostile attitude towards Buddhism and became good friends with many famous monks and learnt much from them. Tales had it that Lu Yu was sent to his ancestral home after his death and buried beside the tomb of his stepfather monk Zhiji, as a compensation for his rebellion in youth.

A tea bowl made by an Imperial kiln of Song Dynasty.

The Book of Tea comprises three volumes, ten sections. The first section—source—deals with origin, name, type, producing place and characteristics of tea. Second section—tool—talks about picking and making tools and using methods of tea. Third section —making—expatiates the time and requirements of picking tea, explains the six steps of making tea, and classifies tea cakes into eight ranks in light of their shape and color. Fourth section—apparatus—records 23 kinds of tea-cooking tools. Fifth section—boiling— tells ways of cooking tea and evaluates water quality. Sixth section—drinking—reviews the history of tea drinking and shows different ways of drinking tea.

A painting of Song Dynasty *Contest of Tea* (part) reflecting competing drinking tea.

Seventh section—history—is the largest part of the book. It collects literature on tea from ancient books, gathers 43 historical figures from ancient times to Tang Dynasty, and compiles 48 legends, anecdotes, fables, and so forth. Eighth section—production—divides tea leaf producing area in the whole country into eight parts, and classifies tea leaves of each part into four grades, with elaborate specifications. Ninth section—omission—discusses which apparatus can be omitted under what conditions in what ways. Tenth section —picture—is about Lu Yu's advocacy of drawing the above content and hanging it on the wall for constant observance to guide one's tea-cooking skill. *The Book of Tea* covers the whole process from tea picking to tea making, and refers to every aspect of tea culture. It can be called an encyclopedia of tea. This book is later translated into several languages and exerts an enormous effect in the world as well. As Lu Yu was gradually apotheosized, tea sellers in later generations put his statue in apparatus, believing that Lu Yu could bless them with a blooming business. Some sold their tea with Lu Yu's statue as a gift. As long as one bought a certain amount of tea, he could get a statue for free.

Cai Xiang and *Record of Tea*

Cai Xiang (1012–1067) was a top politician and tea expert as well as one of the four most successful calligraphers of Song Dynasty. Based on big-dragon tea roll, he invented the delicate looking, meticulously made, and superb tasting small-dragon tea roll, which soon became a nonesuch. Contemporaries exclaimed: gold was easy to get while small-dragon roll was hard to attain. Cai Xiang was expert on tea. Once upon a time, he visited a good friend. The host prepared small-dragon roll for him on purpose, but Cai Xiang said upon the first sip, "there must be big-dragon roll in it." The host immediately blamed the kid-servant who prepared the tea. The servant had only to admit that just now more guests arrived. Not having enough time to prepare tea, he mixed the two

A mural excavated from a burial site of Liao Dynasty reflecting the scene of drinking tea.

一夜尋黃居寀龍不獲方悟半
月前是曹光州借去摹楊更須
一兩月方浮恐王君疑是翻悔
且告子細泝与後取印納也
却寄團茶一餅与之旌其好事
也予嘗 襄

A letter written by Su Shi, a famous litterateur in Song Dynasty, once mentioned tea cake.

kinds of roll together. This story is similar to that of Lu Yu telling water but more credible. Cai Xiang was the inventor of small-dragon roll, so naturally he knew it like the back of his hand. Had the kid-servant known this, he wouldn't have dared to lie in front of Cai Xiang.

Lu Yu's *The Book of Tea* didn't mention the most renowned tea in Song Dynasty-Beiyuan Tea of Fujian Province. Cai Xiang found this a big pity, so he wrote *Record of Tea* to compensate for this. *Record of Tea* consisted of two parts. The first part had ten items, dealing with quality of tea and ways of cooking and drinking. The second part had nine items, talking about apparatus for cooking. Cai Xiang insisted that observing tea with eyes was like physiognomy because the outside told of the inside. Good tea cake was like the face of a healthy person. Its luster, sleekness and compactness were symbols for top-grade quality. Cai Xiang was also for the naturalness of tea and against the practice of adding spices into tea cakes.

Being excellent in calligraphy, Cai Xiang often called for tea to add fun to the pleasure of calligraphy writing. When asked for inscription, he was often given tea as gift. Cai Xiang never lost in any competition in tea. Because of his excellence in tea and calligraphy, his *Record of Tea* transcribed by himself of course became priceless, causing many people's extreme jealousy. The book was eventually stolen by a subordinate who published it in secret. The manuscript being stolen, Cai Xiang felt very sorry. The published *Record of Tea* being full of mistakes, he felt even bitterer. So he had no choice but to spend time rearranging his book. This time he carved the content

Emperor Huizong's painting *Wen Hui Tu* (part) of Song Dynasty has reflected a scene of feast with tea.

on a rock for safety's sake, not having to worry about its being falsified or stolen again.

Zhao Ji and *General Remarks on Tea*

Zhao Ji (Emperor Huizong) was the eighth emperor of Song Dynasty. Though an incompetent emperor, he was a very gifted artist, making tremendous achievements in calligraphy, painting, literature, and other artistic fields as well. The kind of calligraphic style invented by him—Thin *Jin* Style—was a gem in its kind, not only enjoying a high reputation in its own time, but much admired by later generations as well. Emperor Huizong was also a superb painter and tea master. However, it was also through him that the dynasty of Northern Song (960–1127) was overthrown.

Zhao Kuangyin—the first emperor of Song Dynasty—was a military officer at first. He seized his power from the previous

The painting *Tea Meeting at Hui Mountain* by Wen Zhengming of Ming Dynasty.

Dynasty. But to prevent others from following his steps and subverting his kingdom, he gave military power to civil officers who didn't know how to maneuver armies at all. As a result, Song Dynasty's military strength was always fairly weak and it was always under threat from northern ethnic regimes. The situation came to its worst at Emperor Huizong's time. He was the kind of person who lived his life as a kind of art. Completely immerged in artistic charm, he totally ignored the cruelty of reality. When the Nurchen nationality to the northeast of China rapidly rose up and threatened to devour the Song Dynasty, Emperor Huizong mistook it as a flourishing age of "reconstruction from ruin and prosperity of coastal regions" and started compiling his *General Remarks on Tea*. In 1125, Nurchen army invaded Song Dynasty in a big way. Hurriedly passing down the reign to his son, Emperor Huizong thought he could preserve himself this way, but his successor didn't eave the situation, either. In the second year, Nurchen army marched southward again, breaching the capital of Song and capturing thousands of Song people, including Emperor Huizong and his son. Emperor Huizong suffered all kinds of tortures in the foreign land and finally died there.

Emperor Huizong was fond of drinking tea. He drew a picture called *Picture of Drinking Tea*, in which he was dressed in common clothes and enjoyed himself taking and discussing tea with the surrounding ministers. It is recorded in reference books that Emperor Huizong once cooked tea for his ministers in person. His tea had white froth floating on the surface like scarce stars and a brilliant moon. *General Remarks on Tea* is Emperor Huizong's summary of his predecessors' achievements, and is also a summary of his own experience in tea drinking. The book contains merely 2800 words, but is very comprehensive, divided into exordium and 20 catalogues of place, climate, picking, steaming and pressing, making, differentiating, etc. The book has three main points. First, it records and introduces the planting, picking and processing of Beiyuan Tea (produced in today's Jian'ou county of Fujian

The painting *Shi Ming Tu* by Tang Yin of Ming Dynasty.

Province) which represents the highest level of tea making at that time. Second, it introduces how to differentiate tea cakes. Third, it talks about the art of cooking tea and competition in tea. Emperor Huizong maintained that tea picking should be in the morning and stop after sunrise. Tea cakes that met three standards of "sparking in color, dense in texture, and sonorous in grinding" were of top quality. He opposed the partial emphasis on seeds and producing places of tea, and insisted that whether tea was good or not entirely depended on the facility or clumsiness of making techniques but not on the producing place. *General Remarks on Tea* put its stress on the part of competition in tea. His invention of "Seven Round" method of cooking tea was the most complex and delicate tea ceremony skill in Chinese history.

Zhu Quan and *Guide of Tea*

Zhu Quan (1378–1448) was the 17th son of Zhu Yuanzhang—the founder of Ming Dynasty. Since very young Zhu Quan was

brighter than others and was entitled as a prince at the age of 14. Like Emperor Huizong, Zhu Quan failed as a political ruler. His brother Zhu Di (1360–1424) house-arrested him for his throne and didn't release him until he succeeded in his coup and obtained the crown. After that Zhu Quan withdrew from society and devoted himself to Taoism in his later years, living a life free from worldly anxieties.

Zhu Quan's *Guide of Tea* comprises two parts—preface and body, body being subdivided into discussion of tea and catalogue of tea. Discussion of tea copes with tea's functions, introduces five names of tea, and comments on works by earlier scholars. Despite that Zhu Quan highly appraised Lu Yu's *The Book of Tea* and Cai Xiang's *Record of Tea* and considered them the only ones of value among its kind, he put forward different opinions from theirs. Zhu Quan didn't think much of tea cakes popular in Tang and Song dynasties, believing that the practice of "making leaves into powder, grease and cake" stripped tea leaves of their natural taste, whereas cooking loose tea catered for the inherent nature of tea. Zhu Quan

criticized Lu Yu for running after "curiosity" too much. This was in accordance with the trend of loose tea replacing iced tea and cooking method supplanting frying method.

Catalogue of tea includes four ways of drinking tea—tea estimating, water estimating, water boiling and tea cooking, two ways of making tea—collecting and smoking with scent, and ten apparatus—stove, kitchen stove, mill, grain mill, etc. Zhu Quan made many interesting improvements on tea apparatus. Take teaspoon for instance. People of past dynasties used gold, people of Ming Dynasty used silver or copper, but Zhu Quan substituted them with coconut shell. He opposed Song people in using black-glaze porcelain, believing white porcelain could foil the brightness of tea and making it "clear and lovely." He also criticized the contemporary practice of making tea shelves with wood, thinking "mottled bamboo and black bamboo are purest." In short, Zhu Quan was against luxury, triviality and complexity, but was for natural and crude simplicity. He invented methods of making flower tea, suggesting plum blossom, sweet-scented osmanthus, and jasmine because they could add fragrance and loveliness to tea.

The best part in *Record of Tea* is Zhu Quan's definition of atmosphere for drinking tea. For Zhu Quan, tea helped people to be "undisturbed by worldly worries and uplifted from vulgarities," so it was "conducive to virtue cultivation." Therefore, tea should be drunk in tranquil locations, either among springs and rocks, or in pine or bamboo forests, either under a silvery moon on breezy night, or near a bright and clean window. While drinking tea, one should avoid vulgar talk, and should "study metaphysics and seek truth, purify thoughts and elevate mind."

Lu Tingcan and *Additional Book of Tea*

During the hundreds of years from Tang to Qing Dynasty, great changes took place in the producing places of tea, producing

< The painting *Tea-drinking* (part) by Wen Zhengming of Ming Dynasty.

methods of tea, and the apparatus for making and cooking tea. It was at that time that a book about tea appeared, which made ample references and quotation and was also very practical. That was *Additional Book of Tea*.

This book followed the structure of *Book of Tea*, being divided into ten parts—origin of tea, tools of tea, production of tea, apparatus of tea, cooking of tea, drinking of tea, ceremonies of tea, making of tea, general information about tea, and pictures of tea. Making amendments and supplements to many tea books after Tang Dynasty, this book was not only ten times that of *Book of Tea* in volume, but differed very much from it in content, too. It can be called a general summary and comprehensive expression of Chinese ancient tea books. Its author Lu Tingcan was once an official in Wuyi, Fujian Province, which was a perfect place for a scholar fond of tea. He not only took great efforts to study origin of Wuyi tea and understand relevant matters about it, but read widely to accumulate knowledge on tea. He wrote a draft of this book when he was still in his post. After retiring to his hometown, he finished the book and presented to the world in about 1734.

In addition to the said works, two others are worth mentioning —*Biography of Ye Jia* and *On Tea and Wine*. *Biography of Ye Jia* is a biography of tea written by the great poet Su Shi of Song Dynasty. In the book he compared tea to a loyal minister and noble man. *On Tea and Wine* is a dialogue-style article written in personification by scholar Wang Fu of Tang Dynasty. In the book tea and wine had a heated argument in self praising and opponent despising. In the end water came to make peace, arguing that both tea and wine couldn't do without water, so they two had better stop the dispute and strived for mutual development. The article was easy and witty, full of humor, not common in articles with tea as a subject.

The Spread of Tea
from China

An ancient dak on the Tea-Horse Road. Photo by Li Yuxiang.

Tea originated from southwest mountains and took root in regions inhabited by people of Han nationality, widely cultivated and made, whereas ethnic groups living in southwest China had to get tea from Han areas. Wherever tea arrived, it conquered local dwellers with its peculiar fascination, taking an irreplaceable position in their life. Tea was not only a personal taste or a communal habit, but was in direct connection with national security. Since tea became a daily necessity for Han people in Tang Dynasty, all dynasties in the following more than 1,000 years carried out exclusive sale of tea, and tea tax was a mainstay in each Dynasty's fiscal revenues. With its entry into the life of northwest and southwest ethnic groups, it was also widely accepted and loved, so tea became a key factor in dealing with the relation between Han nationality and minor nationalities. After it went out of China into the world market, tea concerned Chinese foreign trade and profoundly affected the foreign affairs and national fortune of China.

The building of the Administration for Tea Affairs of Ming Dynasty in Ya'an, Sichuan Province. Photo by Li Yuxiang.

Tea Tax and Tea Trade System

Tea drinking was very popular in Tang Dynasty. As Old Book of Tang had it, "tea is food, no different than rice and salt. It catches on far and near. It dispels tiredness and appeals to all. Farmers working in the field were particularly fond of it." When tea became "food" "appealing to all," the free trade and enjoyment of tea came to an end. Noticing how important tea was for common folks, the ruling class realized it was a nice means of increasing financial income, so they began levying taxes on tea. In 780, Tang government

The First Producer of Tea
Tea-growing and tea-production have long been a distinctive component of Chinese agriculture. In 2008 more than 1.6 million hectares in China were planted with tea, producing 1.24 million tons, a third of the world's total. In the same year China exported 297,000 tons of tea, with a value of 682 million US dollars, less only than Kenya and Srilanka.

The large-scale horse fair at Er'yuan, Yunnan Province. Photo by Xu Jinyan, provided by *China Tourism*, Hong Kong.

levied tax on tea to augment military budget in order to suppress mutiny, and that was the earliest tea tax. But tea tax then was merely wartime expedient, and was stopped after mutiny was put down. After 16 months, Emperor of the time issued an edict of self-criticism, which showed that the ruling class then didn't think tea tax to be a reasonable measure. Nevertheless, at the end of Tang Dynasty, seeing the successive military chaos, imperial court had to put tea tax in their schedule again, even in an intensified form. Tea was levied according to its weight rather than actual price. Later, authorities implemented full-scale exclusive sale, not only unitively purchasing all tea to be made by government, but taking the cultivation of tea into exclusive possession of government, forcing tea farmers to transplant tea trees and burn their stored tea leaves. Through these measures the Tang government was in full control of the production, processing and circulation of tea and made huge profits. The cultivation and making of tea in Tang Dynasty has reached a certain scale. A large many people of tea areas lived on tea. The completely exclusive sale of tea ridded numerous people of income and caused tremendous public resentment. Tea farmers in a region between Yangtze River and Yellow River announced in public that if the imperial court didn't change its decision, they would launch a rebellion. Fortunately the chancellor who suggested entire inhibition of tea trade was killed then. His successor abolished the old system and adopted partial exclusive sale. From then on, although rulers of different dynasties adopted various policies about tea, tax levying and exclusive sale have always been in action, and was only thoroughly cancelled until the middle of Qing Dynasty.

The barrels used to make Suyou Tea in Tibet. Photo by Xie Guanghui, provided by *China Tourism*, Hong Kong.

Bartering of Tea and Horse

Early Asian nomadic groups considered tea a catholicon that could cure all diseases. People ate tea leaves together with salt, garlic and dried fish, which was like what happened in Europe when tea first arrived there. Like Han nationality, minor nationalities of China also accepted and loved tea. They needed tea leaves from areas under Chinese government's domination, so tea directly concerned the harmony among different nationalities. Dynasties after Tang all governed borderlands through tea, believing that tea was "more powerful than thousands of soldiers." Song Dynasty even tried to force Yuan Hao (1003–1048)—king of Western Xia, a kingdom founded by a minor nationality-to surrender by cutting off its provision of tea.

A part of the Tea–Horse Road among mountains. Photo by Li Yuxiang.

The Potala Palace in Lhasa, the destination of the Ancient Tang-Tibet Road. Photo by Li Yuxiang.

Inland China produced tea leaves while northwest minor nationalities abounded in horses. In early Tang Dynasty, Han people usually exchanged silk for horses from ethnic groups. Tea was not in the major place in the bilateral trade, and leaves got by ethnic groups were only used for nobilities' consumption. After its middle period, Tang Dynasty was busy suppressing incessant insurrections. It needed large amounts of horses, but exchanging horses with silk was a losing proposition, so rulers decided to trade tea leaves for war horses in urgent need. Meanwhile, like in inland China, tea spread from nobilities to plebeians and merged into their lives. A story had it that Tang government wanted to exchange tea for horses with Hui He (a minor nationality in northwest China) but was refused. Hui He didn't want tea leaves but preferred to offer 1,000 horses in exchange for Lu Yu's The Book of Tea. Officials of Tang Dynasty looked all around for this book. In the end poet Pi Rixiu (c.834–883) got one and solved this urgent matter. This story shows that drinking tea has become a fashion among ethnic groups then and tended to be more and more refined. Song, Ming and Qing dynasties after Tang all inherited the business pattern of trading tea for horses, so the history of bartering of tea and horse must have reached over 1,000 years.

The Tang-Tibet Road and the Tea-Horse Road

Sichuan and Yunnan in southwest China are major tea producing areas since ancient time. So some people guess that Tibet, which is near Sichuan and Yunnan, had tea since Han Dynasty. However, the Tibetans, who held Princess Wencheng in high esteem, chose to believe that it was she who brought tea to Tibet. In early years of Tang Dynasty, Songzan Gambo (617–650), who just founded a slavery regime in Tibet, sent envoys to the capital of Tang to pay respect to Emperor Taizong (reign from 626

to 649) and asked for a marriage. Taizong decided to pick a princess in his relatives and married her to Tibet. In 641, the team escorting Princess Wencheng to Tibet set forth from capital Chang'an (today's Xi'An of Shaanxi Province), went along the north bank of River Wei and across Long Mountain to Qinzhou (today's Tianshui of Gansu). Then they went on westward through Hezhou (today's Linxia of Gansu) and the Yellow River until they reached Qinghai. They passed Longzhi to Shancheng (today's Xining of Qinghai), along River Qiang (today's Yaowang River) in the direction of southwest They climbed over Zi Mountain (today's Bayankara Mountain) and went across River Maoniu (today's Tongtian River), past Yushu region and over Dangla Mountain to Nagchu in north Tibet. At last they arrived at the Tibetan capital Lhosa (today's Lhasa), opening a new chapter in the history of amity between Tang and Tibet.

Princess Wencheng brought to Tibet medicine, calendar, vegetable seed, textile and brewing technique, and tea. It is said that on arriving in Tibet, princess Wencheng wasn't accustomed to the climate and diet there. She drank half a cup of milk at breakfast, and drank half a cup of tea to dispel the strong smell. Later she just mixed milk and tea together, adding pine nut core, ghee, etc., thus giving birth to buttered tea, a drink much loved by the Tibetans.

It is recorded in history records that some of the tea leaves introduced to Tibet at that time were produced in Anhui, Zhejiang, Hunan, Hubei and Sichuan. Starting from the time when Princess Wencheng married to Tibet, envoys came back and forth between Tang Dynasty and Tibet, making frequent business. The Tang-Tibet Road quickly flourished in these circumstances. This road is not only for transportation and business between inland China and Qinghai and Tibet since Tang Dynasty, but is the only way from China to Nepal, India and other countries. It has existed for over 1300 years until this day.

The introduction of tea leaves greatly changed the life of the Tibetans. They have folk ballads like this—"food of Han partly fills your stomach while tea of Tibet keeps you full," and "one would

< The ancient Tea-Horse Road on a cliff at Hutiao Gorge, Yunnan Province. Photo by Yang Chubin, provided by *China Tourism*, Hong Kong.

rather starve for three days than not drink tea for one day." This is because the Qinghai-Tibet Plateau is scarce in vegetable and natives there live on meat and milk, while tea does not only help digest but provides necessary vitamins for human body.

In response to the huge need for tea leaves, a trade channel like the Silk Road emerged. Among the mountains and high peaks in the southwest frontier of China, people opened the most beautiful, most dangerous and most exciting road in the world. For thousands of years, innumerable horse teams come and go on this road. This is the historic "Tea-Horse Road." It took its primary shaped in Western Han, when it was called "Shu Shen Du Dao," meaning the road between Sichuan and India in Chinese. With the increasing frequency of business focused on tea leaves, this road bloomed since Tang Dynasty and kept being strengthened in later times, developing into the biggest and most complex business network in the Asian continent.

In history, Tea-Horse Road has had three major trunks—the Tang-Tibet Road (today's Qing (Qinghai)-Zang (Tibet) trunk) and the two lines later called Dian (Yunnan)-Zang (Tibet) trunk and Chuan (Sichuan)-Zang (Tibet) trunk. Dian-Zang line starts from Xishuangbanna and Simao in south Yunnan, through Lincang, Baishan, Dali, Lijiang, Zhongdian and Deqin to Changdu, Linzhi and Lhasa of Tibet. Chuan-Zang line sets out from Ya'an of Sichuan, through Kangding to Changdu to meet Dian-Zang line and then radiates to the whole Tibet through Lhasa. After that tea leaves are sold to the other side of Himalaya—India, Nepal, and other south Asian countries. Among these three Tea-Horse Road, the Tang-Tibet Road developed early. The other two got to be rapidly developed because Tibetans were more and more interested in tea from Sichuan and Yunnan. They were not just for bantering of tea for horses either. Gangs of horse teams shuttled back and forth, dealing in tea leaves and food from Sichuan and Yunnan, medicine and wool of Tibet, and jewelry and spice from India and other countries. To make transportation easier, Yunnan

A suspension bridge on the Ancient Tang-Tibet Road in Northern Tibet. Photo by Li Yuxiang.

tea leaves were mostly made into bricks or blocks, which were tidy and nice and easy to be packaged and loaded. For thousands of years the Tea-Horse Road has become a key band in the cultural, economic and religious blending of all nationalities in Yunnan, Sichuan and Tibetan areas. It has also become a crucial channel for Chinese tea and Chinese culture to be spread to the world, because through the hands of one merchant after another, the Chinese, the Indian, and the Persian carried tea leaves to the faraway West Asia and Europe.

Tea house (on the right) along the Tea Road in Russia.

Inside view of tea yard in Urga, present-day Ulaanbaatar.

Popularization of Tea Leaves in the World

The diffusion of tea from China to the whole world has always been through two means—by sea and by land. Landway includes the tea road to middle Asia, West Asia and Europe that overlapped with the old silk road after Tang Dynasty, the business roads to south Asian countries with the Tang-Tibet Road and the Tea-Horse Road as two major trunks, and a tea road to Russia through the Mongolian Plateau exploited during Ming and Qing dynasties. Seaway consisted of three. One set from tea areas of Jiangsu, Anhui, Zhejiang and Fujian to Japan and the Korean peninsula through Yangzhou and Quanzhou ports in Tang and Song dynasties. Another started from tea areas of Jiangxi, Zhejiang and Fujian to America through Ningbo, Quanzhou and Guangzhou ports and across the Pacific Ocean. The last one went from Nan Yang to America and through India to Europe.

During Song, Yuan and early Ming dynasties, China strictly banned tea, which prevented its popularization. On the 3rd year of Yongle in Ming Dynasty (1405), Zheng He (1371 or 1375–1433 or 1435) went to the west with a huge store of fame tea from various places as gifts. This opened the export of tea leaves in Ming Dynasty. In early Qing Dynasty, since the output of tea leaves increased, the ban was basically cancelled and government permitted civilians to carry on tea business. Before seaway was started, tea groups made up of Shanxi merchants traveled by land. They traveled to Wuyi Mountain to collect tea leaves, "across Fenshui Pass, outside Jiujiang, past Shanxi and Urga (today's Ulaanbaatar) and north to Kiakhta (meaning business city in Chinese, once a major business port in China for Sino-Russian business), covering a distance of nearly 6,000 kilometers and then passed Siberia to Europe. This is the international business road that input Chinese tea to Russia or even the entire Europe, called the Tea Road. When tea leaves were exported to Russia by land, they were not so likely to get damped and went bad as by sea, so leaves arriving in Russia were better in quality than those transported by sea. The leaves to Russia were mostly in the form of tea bricks. Very soon the Russians accepted and loved Chinese tea. As a contemporary writer said, tea has become a requisite in Sino-Russian business because they have got used to drinking Chinese tea and it was hard to give it up.

In 1729, China and Russia signed Kiakhta Frontier Agreement, formally settling Kiakhta as the place where merchants of the two countries could do business, making it an important collecting and distributing place of tea and tea business prospered with speed. At the end of 18th century, the Tea Road witnessed its peak, effectively promoting the business of other goods along the road and pushing the economic communication between China and Europe. On this road, vehicle groups, horse groups and mule groups knew no end. When it came to the 1830s, exportation of tea leaves accounted for 93% of the Sino-Russian trade volume.

The popularization of tea in Britain didn't differ much from that of other countries, also from royal families and nobilities to common folks, and tea leaves quickly became a necessary in the daily life of British people. Britain started importing tea leaves from China by sea since 1637, when British merchant ships arrived at Humen, Guangzhou, and took 112 pounds of tea leaves. At first tea leaves imported to Britain were mostly green tea, but because their quality couldn't be guaranteed, black tea leaves took their place, which directly affected the tea-drinking habit of British people.

British demand for tea grew bigger and bigger and Sino-British trade gradually came to focus on tea. Because of its huge request for tea leaves, Britain suffered an annually larger trade deficit in its trade with China. At the end of 18th century, Britain spent 40,000 Liang silver to import tea leaves from China through East India Company every year. It exported woolen goods, metallic goods and cotton to China too, but the total worth of those three items only amounted to 1/6 of the worth of tea. British merchant ships were often loaded with silver to purchase tea leaves in Guangzhou.

In order to change this situation, Britain levied heavy import tax on tea leaves, keeping the tax rate over 100% from 1806 to 1833. Meanwhile, East India Company was actively seeking other sources for tea. However, at that time very few places other than China produced tea, and China banned exportation of tea seeds and tea-making techniques for the sake of interest protection. In 1834, Bentinck—British governor in India organized a tea committee to study the possibility of planting Chinese tea in India. Due to the fact that Qing government forbade foreigners from entering China, Gordan—the committee secretary came to China in disguise and managed to buy large amounts of tea seeds in Wuyi Mountain, which were secretly shipped to Calcutta in 1835 and were cultivated to 42,000 tea tree saplings, scattered in Assam, Kumaon etc.Later the committee invited Chinese tea master to produce the first batch of finished tea (8 boxes) with the technique of Wuyi Rock tea in 1838. Those were shipped to London and made quite a sensation in the government as well as the public, laying the foundation for tea industry in India who is the number 1 tea-producing country in the world now. In 1867, offspring of those tea trees were introduced to Sri-Lanka and made it the 3rd tea-producing country in the future. Since the 1860s, Chinese tea was confronted with the competition from tea of India and Ceylon in world market. Its market share shrank little by little and lost its dominance completely in the 1880s, whereas India became the biggest supplier of tea leaves.

Chinese export of tea leaves to Britain gained China a large trade surplus, so British government ordered its East India Company to carry opium to China in secret, so that Sino—British trade was basically reversed. To prevent silver from outflowing, Qing government implemented a policy of banning opium-smoking and opium trade, severely attacking opium importation. This is the immediate reason for the breaking out of the Opium War between China and Britain in 1840. After the war, as the winner, Britain asked for "business at five ports," two of which were in Fujian. Britain's aim was still to control the tea areas in Fujian. Wuyi tea went on being import in large amount through Xiamen, Fuzhou and Guangzhou ports. Under the blow of the "business at five ports," road of tea leaves that sold to the north was replaced by the "sea road of tea leaves." Shanxi business groups dealing in Wuyi tea dispersed. After the Opium War, China lost its sovereignty and territory day by day, starting its 100-year-long history of humiliation.

Similarly, another world—changing war was also related to tea and Britain. Tea leaves imported from China to Britain were further sold to other places, and North America was the largest market for the entrepot trade of tea leaves. Britain levied special tax on tea leaves in its northern America colonies and sold its unsalable tea leaves there, which caused fierce resistance. In 1773, "Boston Tea Party" members took hold of three tea ships of East India Company and sank 342 boxes of tea leaves worth 18,000 pounds to the bottom of sea for ever. "Boston Tea Incident" was a fuse for the American Independent War, and the tea that was sunk was the long-reputed Chinese Wuyi tea. After America obtained its independence, Sino-American tea trade thrived for a while. Americans exchanged ginseng, sealskin and sandalwood for tea leaves in Guangzhou, and took the leaves back to America for sale. A number of people became millionaires in this way. In coastal areas of America, many people dreamed of getting rich through tea trade in China. As long as they got a sailboat that could contain five people, they planned to sail to Guangzhou to import tea.

The Opium War and Independent War of North America were all related with tea. The tiny leaves calmly and quietly changed the power structure of the world. Nevertheless, while the Opium War led to the accumulated poverty and weakness of a 1,000-year-old country, the latter signified the rising up of a modern power. What is implied in this is well worth the consideration of everyone.

Lingering Taste of Famous Teas

China has 16 Provinces that produce tea, including Taiwan. From boiling tea as soup, to making it into tea cakes, and to make tea with full leaves, Chinese people have passed a long period in their study and usage of tea. Either by accident or on purpose, they continually discovered and modified new methods of making tea, thus deriving different kinds of tea. Because of the different producing methods, people generally categorize Chinese tea into six major types—green tea, black tea, oolong tea, white tea, yellow tea and dark tea. Besides, there are processed sorts such as jasmine tea, compressed tea, etc. Each type has its representative "celebrity tea," and each "celebrity tea" has its irreplaceable appearance and scent, some even have beautiful legends. The so—called famous teas renowned for their top quality in color, fragrance as well taste are mostly the combining result of excellent natural condition, top class breed of tea trees, refined picking methods, and exquisite processing technique.

Green Tea

Green tea is the oldest type of tea in China. It is also the tea with the largest output in China. Many Provinces and cities are renowned for their production of green tea, the most eminent ones being Zhejiang, Jiangxi and Anhui. Green tea leaves haven't been fermented, so they largely retain the original flavor of tea, which is simple, elegant and lasting. On first sip, green tea tastes a little thin. But on appreciating it, you will find its fragrance flowing in your mouth and reluctant to leave. To make green tea, we mainly use the methods of steaming green, frying green and sunning green, respectively using steaming,

Tribute Tea

'Tribute tea' was new tea contributed by tea-producing regions to the ancient imperial court for use there. Systematic regulations for tribute tea appeared first in Tang dynasty, and reached their full development under the Song. Tribute tea was top quality tea which had been selected extremely carefully, and for this reason many of China's famous teas have been selected for palace use at some stage in their history. At the time of the Qingming festival each year newly picked tribute tea had to be transported to the capital. In Northern Song times a special official visited tribute tea regions to oversee production of tribute tea, the tea pressed into disks with molds bearing a dragon or phoenix shape, which was popularly referred to as 'Dragon-phoenix ball tea'. Records show that just the Jianxi region of Fujian alone sent as many as 47 thousand pounds of tribute tea to the imperial court in one year, a clear sign of how much tea the court needed—the tea was not only consumed by members of the court, but also played an important role as an imperial gift.

< The name of Longjing tea comes from the well beside West lake. Photo by Li Yuxiang.

The tea garden at Longjing Village. Photo by Li Yuxiang.

frying and sunning to get rid of the moisture in fresh tea leaves and bring out their fragrance. The water shouldn't be too hot when making green tea, favorably 80°C. First soak the leaves in a little warm water, then fill the cup full. Only put on the lid for one or two minutes, otherwise the taste would be affected. Or you can first prepare a glass of warm water and then put leaves into it.

West Lake Longjing Tea

West Lake lies in Hangzhou, Zhejiang Province. Hangzhou is one of the most beautiful cities of China, enjoying a high fame since ancient times. It is, together with Suzhou of Jiangsu Province, regarded as the paradise under sky and heaven on earth. West Lake is the most celebrated scenic spot of Hangzhou. It makes a big contribution to bring Hangzhou its enormous fame and it is also why West Lake Longjing tea gets its name. Hangzhou is surrounded by mountains in three sides. As early as the Tang Dynasty, Tianzhu Temple and Lingyin Temple in the West Lake area already made tea. Longjing was called Longhong in early times. In the Ming Dynasty, local people found a dragon-shaped rock when digging a well, so the name of Longjing came into being (*Jing* means a well in Chinese). After its appearance, Longjing tea rose to fame quickly and soon became one of the fame teas. Known for being fresh and tender, the best Longjing leaves should be picked and processed before Pure Brightness (a day around April 5th or 6th), called before-brightness tea. Leaves picked and processed after Pure Brightness and before Grain Rain were a little worse in quality, called before-rain tea. According to the various

It's time to pick up Longjing tea leaves when spring is coming to West lake. Photo by Li Yuxiang.

New Longjing tea. Photo by Li Yuxiang.

Flosses on the new-grown Longjing tea leaves. Photo by Li Yuxiang.

shapes of the leaves, people gave them different fancy names. The carefully selected leave shoots were Lotus Heart. One-shoot-one-piece leaves were Banner Spear. One-shoot-two-piece leaves were Sparrow Tongue. West Lake Longjing has always been known for four typical features—green in color, strong in fragrance, sweet in taste, and beautiful in shape. After being made, the leaves stretched out, straightened themselves and swam up and down in the water, displaying a lively picture. The tea was clear and clean, and left a pleasant and long aftertaste.

There is an interesting tale about West Lake Longjing. When Emperor Qianlong of Qing Dynasty went to the south, he went to the West Lake district to have a drink of local Longjing tea. Seeing the skillfulness of the tea-picking girls, he couldn't help getting interested and started learning to pick. Just then, some attendants hurried along to announce that the Queen Mother was ill. Carelessly putting the newly picked leaves in his sleeve, Qianlong hurried back to Beijing. The Queen Mother had nothing serious, just a little indigestion, plus missing her son. With the son's coming

Tea soup made from new Longjing tea. Photo by Li Yuxiang.

back, the Queen Mother got half well. She noticed that gusts of fragrance came out of Qianlong and asked why. Only then did the emperor remember the leaves in his sleeve. He took them out and made tea with them. The tea was sweet, strong and tasteful, curing the Queen Mother's ailment at once. Qianlong was so pleased with this that he gave orders that the 18 tea trees in front of Longjing Temple be named "Royal Tea," which made Longjing tea even more famous. Because the leaves that Qianlong took back to Beijing were pressed flat in his sleeve, the later leaves were all made into that shape.

Picking Longjing involves a lot of knowledge and skill. Tea picking is closely related to seasons. Farmers in tea areas often say that, "three days earlier, it's a treasure. Three days later, it's trash." Generally speaking, the annual picking period lasts 190 to 200 days. Leaves on a tea tree need 22 times of picking a year. Spring tea leaves are picked around late March, when little buds

"Sunning green" for making Longjing tea. Photo by Li Yuxiang.

start to pop out. They want 8 to 9 times of picking because if it's good weather, new leaves will come out in less than 3 days after the previous picking. Only after 8 to 9 times of picking do the leaves come to dormancy. However, in early summer, they wake up and give birth to new leaves again, which are called "Second Tea." Picked leaves must be no longer than 2 centimeters. Two things need to be noticed in picking. First, avoid broken leaves. Second, keep the young leaves, because they will germinate again, and then one young leaf will become two new leaves, and two become four. While picking, both hands and eyes are busily engaged. Leaves on protruding branches will be picked from bottom up alternatively. When picking clumps of different height, you have to stand at one time and squat at another. On sunny days, the newly picked, fresh, tender leaves will have to be put in the basket in time. Seen in a distance, the quick and deft hands of the tea-picking girls are like pairs of butterflies flying among the green leaves. What a wonderful scene!

Picking decides the grades of the leaves, while frying decides their color, shape, and taste. In the past, wood fire or coal fire was used in frying leaves, so heating was very important. There was a saying of "70% of heating and 30% of frying." But now electric cooker is widely used in order to better control the temperature. The procedures of frying Longjing tea is very complex, including shaking, stripping, swinging, tossing, rubbing, knocking, scratching, pressing, grinding, squeezing, etc. Longjing frying is divided into two parts—primary and finishing. The primary part is a process of putting the leaves into a rough shape. The cooker temperature is first high and then low, kept between 240°C and 300°C. The hand movement mainly involves scratching and shaking. After reducing some water, pressing, shaking and swinging procedures are used to primarily shape the leaves. The pressure changes from light to heavy, until leaves are straightened and flattened. After about 12 or 15 minutes, when leaves are 70% or 80% dry, they will be got out of the cooker. Leaves fried at a time weigh about 120 grams. The aim of the finishing part is to further shape and dry the leaves. Normally four cookers of leaves in the primary part go to one cooker in the finishing process, with the temperature around 100°C for 20 to 25 minutes. Hands gradually add force, mainly using scratching, knocking, grinding, pressing, pushing, and other procedures. Each frying process involves only a small amount of leaves but requires a long time. A skilled expert can only fry 1 kilo of dried leaves. Although presently leaves are also fried by machines, these leaves cannot be compared with the hand-fried leaves either in appearance, color or taste. Therefore, first-class West Lake Longjing tea leaves are still fried by hand. This craft usually runs in the family, handed from one generation to another. Tea frying is arduous work. Hands can't touch the cooker bottom but have to contact the leaves' surface, whose temperature is about 60°C. It's ineluctable for learners to get their hands burned. Only after a year of frying, when both hands are covered with thick callus, can they bear the heat in the cooker. Frying is also a practice that needs power of understanding and creativity. Ways of frying vary according to types of tea leaves, water content, cooker temperature, and the size and strength of hands. All these require a lot of thinking. What is more, they require constant accumulation of experiences through practice. The older generation of tea frying workers usually started their apprenticeship since teens. They began with tending the kitchen fire. After 20 or 30 years of training and practice, they finally acquire maturity in their skills. Nevertheless, whether one can become a superb master of tea frying depends on one's talent as well as diligence.

Longjing tea mainly comes from five districts near the West Lake. They used to be classified into five types because of their different producing areas—lion, dragon, cloud, tiger and plum. Now they are combined into three—lion, plum and dragon, of which the most precious are the leaves from the 18 tea trees that had been conferred by Emperor Qianlong. In an auction held in China in 2005, the trigger price for 100 grams of such royal leaves was 80,000 RMB, and the knock-down price was 145,600 RMB per 100 grams, much more valuable than gold.

It's best to use the water from tiger-running spring in Hangzhou when drinking Longjing tea. The spring water, springing from sandstone and quartz sand, is luscious and clear, with high water molecular consistency and surface tension, and low calcium carbonate content. It's also better to choose transparent glasses in order that the stretching and rolling of the leaves in water can be better observed. The rate between the amount of leaves and of water is about 1 to 50. First, pour water into the glass to 1/4 full to wet and immerse the shoots and to feed the dry leaves with water to have them unfold. When fragrance starts to pervade, pour water from a higher position to let the water drop straight into the glass. Use the power of your wrist to raise and lower the pot three times, thus setting the leaves stirring in the water. This tea-cooking method—known as Phoenix Nods Three Times—assures that the leaves have thorough contact with water. It is also to show respect to the guest because "nodding three times" means to bow and salute. This elegant gesture demonstrates the respect for both the guest and tea ceremony. Longjing leaves can be made three times, the second-time tea tasting the best.

Maojian of Mount Huangshan Mount Huangshan is situated in Anhui Province, China. It has topped other famous mountains since ancient times. The great tourist Xu Xiake (1586–1641) of Ming Dynasty, after visiting Mount Huangshan, exclaimed, "there's nothing like Mount Huangshan of Anhui in the whole world. Compared to Mount Huangshan, no other mountain is great enough." Mount Huangshan is made up of a lot of peaks and ridges, 77 of which are over 1,000 meters high. The four most celebrated sights are: rare pines, strange rocks, hot spring, and Cloud Sea, known as "Four Specialties of Mount Huangshan." The tea leaf of Maojian of Mount Huangshan has a light yellow in its verdure. The leaf is covered with white hairs, and the shoot tip is shaped like a mount peak. That's how the name comes into being. After being cooked, the water is clear and bright with a touch of apricot yellow. It tastes strong and fresh and pure. The best Maojian tea leaves an aftertaste even after being cooked five or six times.

Pilochun Pilochun comes from Mount Dongting of Wu County in Suzhou, Jiangsu Province, so it is also called "Dongting Pilochun." Its special feature is its luscious fragrance, so the tea is once called by the local citizens as "frightening fragrance." In Qing Dynasty when Emperor Qianlong visited south China, local officers treated him with this kind of tea. When Qianlong lifted the tea cup, a strong fragrance flew into his nose even before he drank the tea. After drinking it, Qianlong said that it sure deserved its reputation. But finding its name not elegant enough, Qianlong personally gave it the beautiful name of Pilochun. Pilochun looks verdant and like a trumpet shell, with fine and dense flosses around the circumference. It's best to use glasses when drinking Pilochun, because the tea leaves unfold themselves slowly after absorbing water. When they sink and float in the water, their white hairs can be observed vividly, like snow flying in the wind. Pilochun not only gives people pleasure in smell and taste, but gives visual enjoyment as well.

"Sunning green" for making Pilochun tea. Photo by Li Yuxiang.

Famous tea needs famous spring to match with. Here is Huqiu Spring of Suzhou. Photo by Li Yuxiang.

Sweet Dew of Mengding (meaning the top of Mount Mengshan) Sichuan Province is where tea culture is in its height. Many well-known teas stem there, and Sweet Dew of Mengding is one of them. Mount Mengshan lies across Mingshan county and Ya'an county of Sichuan Province. Its five peaks huddle together like a lotus. The mid-peak, which is the highest, has a piece of flat ground on its top, and Sweet Dew of Mengding originates here. As the legend goes, an eminent monk called Ganlu (meaning sweet dew) in Western Han, for the welfare of all, planted tea trees on the mount top with his own hands. That's how Sweet Dew of Mengding got its name. It is one of the most time-honored well-known teas in China, and was honored as the head of tribute teas as early as Tang Dynasty. As the tea is associated with Buddhism, it has been regarded as celestial tea. It is said that once a monk got sick, he met another old monk who told him to pick as many as tea leaves of Mengding within three days around vernal equinox when spring thunders started in action. One *Liang* (a unit of measurement, about 1/20 kilo) can cure chronic disease, two Liang can keep him healthy forever, three Liang can remold him thoroughly, and four Liang can elevate him to be immortal. The sick monk followed the old monk's instruction. He picked one Liang of leaves and his illness went immediately. Even his appearance changed young. Sweet Dew of Mengding is tenderly green and moist, tasting better with second cooking. It is recommended and loved by a great many people.

Black Tea

Black tea is a kind of fermented tea, originating from green tea after it is mixed, kneaded, fermented, dried, and otherwise processed. The water of green tea is freshly green while that of black tea is orange red. But this difference is only skin-deep. What is more important is that black tea doesn't undergo the processes of steaming green or frying green, but is fermented, during which

The tea garden for Qimen Gongfu tea. Photo by Li Yuxiang.

The Qinmen Gongfu tea after fermenting and drying. Photo by Li Yuxiang.

time the tea leaves go through chemical reactions—tea phenol reduced over 90% and tea yellow element and red element being produced. If these two elements are in a right proportion, the water's color will be red and bright. While green tea retains the thin and freshening flavor of the leaves, the fermented black tea gives a stronger and thicker flavor. Black tea first appeared in Qing Dynasty, much younger than green tea. But it occupied an important position in China's foreign trade at the end of Qing Dynasty, with the largest amount of all kinds of tea that were exported to Europe and America.

Black tea originated in Fujian and its vicinities, and later spread to other provinces in the south. At present, black tea is the most produced and most widely drunk tea. It can be divided into three groups: Kungfu black tea, small piece black tea, and broken black tea. Broken black tea a new type developed in India to which the black tea produced in Sri Lanka also belongs. China started to trial produce this group in the 1950s. Small piece black tea is the earliest black tea in China, produced near Fujian (southeast coast of China) and Chong'an. Gongfu black tea is a Chinese specialty developed on the basis of small piece black tea, and is also the most representative black tea of China. Considering the different origins of Chinese Gongfu black tea, they are divided into Qimen Gongfu of Anhui, Dianhong Gongfu of Yunnan, Ninghong Gongfu of Jiangxi, Minhong Gongfu of Fujian, etc.

< The gate to Mount Mengshan. Photo by Li Yuxiang.

Qimen Gongfu Qimen Gongfu tea has a history of over 100 years. In late Qing Dynasty, a retired officer from Fujian brought the making method of black tea back to his hometown Anhui. He set up a Qimen Teahouse, improved small piece black tea, and created a unique Qimen Gongfu black tea. Leaves of this kind of tea should be picked around Clear and Bright, and should go through two major processes of primary making and refining. After primary making, newly picked leaves become crude tea, which should be assorted according to their weight, color and shape. This assortment is the refining process. Qimen Gongfu black tea requires a very particular making process—baked in a sealed room and heated with low temperature to bring out the fragrance of the leaves. The color of this tea is jet black with a bit gray praised as "precious light." Cooked, the water is bright, red and fragrant, with a lingering aftertaste. With different processes, there are different flavors such as honey flavor, flower flavor and fruit flavor, known as "Qimen flavor."

Oolong Tea

Oolong tea is also called green tea. It uses green tea's finishing technique as well as black tea's fermenting skill, so it is a semi-fermented tea between green tea and black tea. For the same reason, it keeps both green tea's and black tea's characteristics–the freshening and clearing flavor of green tea and the thick and luscious fragrance of black tea. The appearance of oolong tea also combines the features of green tea and black tea—verdant leaves with crimson edges. The leaves are in the shape of long cables, bigger and fatter than green tea or black tea after being cooked. These leaves taste strong and thick, so they can be cooked many times. Chinese oolong tea mainly comes from Fujian, Guangdong, Taiwan, etc. Fujian has been the hometown of tea since early time. Most tribute tea came from Fujian in Song Dynasty, including the famous Dragon & Phoenix Cake. Therefore, many people believe that Dragon & Phoenix Cake is the predecessor of oolong tea.

Tie Guanyin Tie Guanyin is produced in Anxi County of Fujian Province, so people often call it "Anxi Tie Guanyin." Anxi is located in the southeast side of the hill, where over 50 kinds of tea leaves are produced, with Tie Guanyin on the top.

Oolong tea.

Another name for Guanyin is Guanshiyin, the most popular female Buddha in China. Chinese folks think she is most charitable and most willing to help people, so they call her "the charitable Guanshiyin Buddha who helps the needy and relieves the distressed." The word "Guanyin" means to listen to people's miseries. It is said that there used to be an old man who devotedly believed in Guanyin. He consecrated green tea in front of Guanyin's shrine every morning and evening for dozens of years on end. One day, he dreamed of himself discovering an unusual tea tree in the crack of a rock near a stream. Just when he was trying to pick its leaves, he was woken up by a barking dog. Waking up, he went to the place he dreamed of. Sure enough, he found a tea tree there and transplanted it to his home, whose leaves gave off tremendous fragrance. What with this tea tree was discovered under the guidance of Guanyin Buddha, and with the leaves were black, moist, burly and weighing like steel, the tree was called Tie (meaning steel) Guanyin because of its sweet smell and beautiful appearance which were characteristic of Guanyin. Whether this story is true or not is beyond proof, but the fact that people used "Guanyin" to name a tea is solid proof of people's fondness of Tie Guanyin.

The tea trees that give birth to Tie Guanyin are born delicate and weak, unable to bear difficult

(Top) The tea garden in Wuyi Mountain, Fujian Province. Photo by Wang Miao, provided by *China Tourism*, Hong Kong.

(Bottom) The tea-making workshop in Anxi Tea Factory, Quanzhou, Fujian Province. Photo by Liu Jiaxiang, provided by *China Tourism*, Hong Kong.

situations. That's why they are said to be "good to drink but hard to plant." The trees germinate in late March every year and their leaves can be picked in early May. Picking time runs throughout spring, summer, autumn and winter, with spring leaves having the largest amount and autumn leaves being the most fragrant. It's best to pick Tie Guanyin from 9 a.m. to 4 p.m. Otherwise the leaves are less tasteful.

Tie Guanyin should be cooked with boiling water, so that its fragrance can be fully brought out. To drink Tie Guanyin involves a lot of knowledge, which can be summarized into six steps—observing, listening, viewing, smelling, tasting, and appreciating.

Observing: high-quality Tie Guanyin leaves are curly, strong, and heavy, with its tip like dragonfly's head, body like a spire, and bottom like frog's leg. Good Tie Guanyin leaves are covered with a thin layer of hoar frost called "sand green." For Tie Guanyin leaves have to be wrapped up with white cloth after finished. They are kneaded and twisted in the cloth so the leaves will shrink. After baked and kneaded many times, the leaves are dried and lightly heated in slow fire. This sublimates the theine in the leaves, which gathers on the leave surface to form the hoar frost. Tie Guanyin also has to be assorted after being made. The common leaves are called crude tea while the good ones are called refined tea. The decisive difference between crude tea and refined tea is the existence of peduncle. Those without it are refined tea while those with it are crude tea.

Listening: Tie Guanyin is usually kneaded about 11 times when they are wrapped in the cloth, sometimes as many as 25 times. Therefore, the leaves are twisted, tight, heavy and massive. Dropped into the tea pot, those leaves that can make ringing sound are good while the common ones can only make husky sound.

Viewing: the water of Tie Guanyin is golden, thick and clear in color. The leaves are fat and bright after cooked, with silk-like sheen on the surface. If the water takes on a dark color with a touch of red, that means the leaves are not very good.

Smelling: when cooked, top Tie Guanyin gives off fragrance like sweet-scented osmanthus,' with a remote flavor chestnut. This is the biggest difference between Tie Guanyin and other oolong teas.

Tasting: Tie Guanyin is not for gulp, but should be sipped little by little. The tongue moves slowly in the mouth to get thorough contact with tea. Then the water gradually flows down the throat to let its deliciousness be fully absorbed.

Appreciating: the most special trait of Tie Guanyin is its Guanyin charm, which refers to its unique taste as opposed to other teas. This charm includes the above five steps. It is a perfect combination of human feeling and tea ceremony and a comprehensive experience of senses and intelligence, possible to be understood by heart but not so probable to communicate with words.

Tie Guanyin contains over 30 mineral elements, of which the contents of potassium, fluorine and especially selenium are the highest. These mineral elements can stimulate the creation of immune protein and antibody, strengthen human ability of preventing disease, and have some effects on coronary heart disease. Besides, Tie Guanyin has over 70 kinds of fragrance, 10 of which are highly characteristic. These smells also have positive effects in relaxing body and heart, as well as health preservation and protection.

Wuyi Rock Tea Wuyi Rock tea is a general name for oolong tea produced in Wuyi Mountain of Fujian. It is the most well known oolong tea whose production is highly delicate, especially the reputed technique of "shaking green." After the fresh leaves are picked, they have to be sunned and slightly adjusted. Then they are thinly spread out on a dustpan and shaken with hands. The edges of the leaves rub with each other, and are oxidized by air after the edges break, so they will turn red. Red Robe is the best type of Wuyi Rock tea and has had a history of over 300 years. Now there are only three Red Robe tea trees. They are over 1,000 years old and live on the cliffs of Wuyi Mountain. The leaf tips are a little red. See from a distance, they look like brilliant red brocade, and this gives it the name of Red Robe. Red Robe leaves are picked every spring. People have to set up scaling ladders to pick a small amount of leaves, so they are extremely precious and valuable.

Fenghuang Dancong (Phoenix Mountain Select) tea is one of the three great varieties of Oolong tea, equal in fame to two other Oolong teas, the tea from the slopes of Wuyi Mountain and Tieguanyin tea from Anxi. In terms of their distinct flavours, Wuyi tea has a rich and mellow fragrance and a long aftertaste; Anxi Tieguanyin is sweetly aromatic and has a sweet, clean flavour; Fenghuang Dancong has a strong aroma and a pronounced, rich taste. Fenghuang Dancong comes from Phoenix Mountain, near Chaozhou city in the eastern part of Guangdong province. Some of the cultivated tea bushes there are as much as 600 years old, and there are many bushes more than 200 years old. So if Chinese who originate from the Chaozhou / Shantou region have a liking for gongfu tea (tea ceremoniously brewed and served in a particular style), this is not unrelated to the fact that their homeland produces a famous old tea, Fenghuang Dancong.

Dark Tea

Green tea is precious for its freshness and tenderness. People usually pick the shoot tips or one-shoot-one-piece leaves as material, because leaves become inferior or bad when they grow up. But this is not always the case. With oolong tea people choose one-shoot-three-or-four-piece leaves. Dark tea is even more special because with it, the rough old one-shoot-five-or-six-piece leaves are selected. But dark tea has its own indispensable characteristics and is also loved by lots of people.

Dark tea is invented by accident. In history, in order to meet northwest ethnic groups' requirements for tea, leaves produced

Tight-pressed tea with various shapes. Photo by Xu Jinyan, provided by *China Tourism*, Hong Kong.

in Yunnan, Sichuan, Hubei, Hunan, and other places have to be transported to the north by sea, and then to the northwest through the Silk Road. In ship cabins, on horse backs, the tea leaves go a very long way and are greatly influenced by weather. Since the leaves are damped and then dried, their chemical elements undergo enormous changes and their color turns blackish brown, too. In spite of this, they still give off rare fragrance, and is quickly spread among the minor groups.

Dark tea belongs to the fermented kind. After the leaves are finished, kneaded and twisted, they have to be gathered and sprinkled with water to be fermented, and at last dried. The water of dark tea is like amber, yellow with a little red. It tastes pure and delicious. Unlike green tea, dark tea uses the rough old leaves as raw material. Also unlike green tea which can't be put aside for a long time, dark tea tastes better with the passage of time. Dark tea can be cooked for many times, which is, again, different from green tea whose taste is a lot worse after twice or three times of cooking. Pu'er tea and Six Castle tea are precious species in the field of dark tea.

Pu'er tea Pu'er tea is a special kind of leaves produced in Yunnan Province, with a history of more than 2,000 years. It is a roll tea. Because of Zhu Yuanzhang's effort to promote this kind of tea in Ming Dynasty, roll tea was gradually replaced by loose tea, but with the exception of Pu'er. Not only didn't Pu'er disappear in time, but it exerted more and more vitality as time went by. Qing Dynasty graded Pu'er as tribute tea and decreed that 33,000 kilos of Pu'er should be handed in every year. Contemporary royalties and celebrities all took pride in collecting and tasting Pu'er tea. It is very good for health care, especially in helping digestion. When spread abroad, Pu'er tea enjoyed a warm welcome and was named "Longevity Tea." Even the great Russian writer Tolstoy has mentioned the magical tea leaves in his *War and Peace*.

Pu'er tea can be roughly divided into two groups. The first group is made through simple sunning, usually known as "Raw

Pu'er." The other kind is made with the technique of "heating pile" (to sprinkle water over a pile of leaves and make them ferment), usually known as "Ripe Pu'er." The greatest fascination of Pu'er tea is that the longer it is preserved, the better it tastes. Generally speaking, raw Pu'er tastes best after about ten years of preservation,

Newly-grown leaves of Pu'er Tea. Photo by Xu Yunhua, provided by *China Tourism*, Hong Kong.

The roll tea made by Xiaguan Tea Factory of Dali, Yunnan Province. Photo by Gao Zhiqiang, provided by *China Tourism*, Hong Kong.

while ripe Pu'er best exerts its fragrance after two or three years of preservation. This feature of Pu'er is similar to that of wine. A bar of 3-gram Pu'er tea which has been preserved for over 60 years was once auctioned as high as more than 10,000 RMB. Pu'er tea is better to be preserved long, but long-year Pu'er costs too much, so many people choose to buy new Pu'er, preserve them, and drink them after many years. Some people even start doing business on Pu'er tea because of this. They purchase tons of Pu'er tea, preserve them, and wait for them to increase in value years later. This is almost the same as those Europeans who invest in grape wine.

Pu'er tea differs sharply in price because of their difference in

< (Top) Lijiang of Yunnan Province, an important town on the Tea-Horse Road. Photo by Li Yuxiang. (Bottom) Xishuangbanna (Sipsongpanna) of Yunnan Province teems with Pu'er tea. Photo by Li Yuxiang.

age. So how to differentiate them becomes a key question. Pu'er leaves are strip-shaped, each leaf having orderly lines. If the lines are irregular, then it is inferior in quality. Standard Pu'er has the color of pork liver, with a bit red in its blackness and with bright luster. The leaves are full and soft. The bottom of ripe leaves is usually the color of dark chestnut because of fermenting. If fermenting goes a littler further, the leaves will be dry, thin, old and hard, with obvious carbonization as if it has been burned in raging fire. Ripe Pu'er smells like ripe tea, while raw Pu'er of over 10 years has a thick fragrance. The tea water is supposed to be clear and bright after leaves are cooked, with oil-like membrane floating on the surface and the bottom of leaves complete and soft. Low-quality Pu'er will be blackish after cooked while good-quality Pu'er is supposed to have lush fragrance when tasted.

The cooking of Pu'er also involves a lot of skills. First, an opener made from hard wood or hard bamboo is used to strip the leaves lay by layer to avoid causing crumbles. The opened Pu'er leaves should be preserved for two weeks before cooked and drunk because then it tastes better. The tea pot is better to be big to prevent heat from dissipating too quickly. Water temperature differs with different types of leaves. Cake tea, brick tea, tight tea or old tea made from crude materials are better to be cooked in boiling water, while high-level shoot tea from tenderer materials should be cooked in lower temperature. The first round is to wash tea and stir its feature, and the water must be thrown away before long. The second round can be tasted carefully. After the second round, each round should extend in time. When the color of the water becomes clear, and the taste becomes thin, new boiling water should be added. This time the tea must be drunk after half an hour. This is the last round and is also the round with the essence of Pu'er. If you are not willing to throw away the remaining leaves, boil them in a pan and they can still emit some last fragrance. Keep in mind that when you throw the tea, only 50% or 60% of the water is poured out at a time. The left water can be further used to release the fragrance of the leaves more thoroughly.

Yellow Tea

Like dark tea, yellow tea was also found by chance when making green tea. People discover that if leaves are not dried in time after being finished, kneaded and twisted, they will turn yellow in color, thus comes the name of yellow tea. At first, people took yellow tea as bad-quality green tea. Yet since people have different taste, many people prefer the savor of yellow tea, which makes yellow tea become one of the six major teas. Yellow tea belongs to fermented tea, and the fermenting process is called "annealing yellow." Junshan Silver Needle of Hunan and Mengdi Yellow Shoot of Sichuan are two representatives of yellow tea. Silver Needle leaves stand straight after being cooked and only subside to the bottom after times of floating and sinking. Being one of the ten top teas of China, Silver Needle leaves are like bamboo shoots breaking out of the soil or spears drawn out of the sheath, both beautiful and delicious.

White Tea

White tea is slightly fermented, only involving adjustment and drying processes. "Three White" should be observed when picking white tea leaves. "Three White" means the one shoot and two leaves should all be covered with white hairs. Leaves made this way are white all over, which gives rise to the name of white tea. In Tang and Song dynasties, people regarded white tea as very valuable, but at that time, white tea was just a rare kind of tea tree whose leaves were white, not the white tea we know today. White Hair Silver Needle and White Peony produced in Fujian are representatives of white tea.

In addition to the above six major types of tea, there are also Tight-pressed tea and Scented tea produced by re-processing

White Hair Silver Needle tea (a kind of white tea) of Fujian Province.

the leaves. Tight-pressed tea comes from tight pressing crude tea leaves after steaming them in high temperature. This kind of tea can be divided into tea cake, tea brick, tea roll and other groups according to their shape. Tuo tea of Yunnan outstands in this kind. Scented tea, with its history of over 1,000 years, comes from drinking edible flowers and tea leaves together. People in Qing Dynasty liked making scented tea themselves. They spread crumbled calcium oxide at the jar bottom, cover it with two layers of bamboo leaves, and heap flowers on the bamboo leaves. The calcium oxide is highly water absorptive, so it can absorb the water contained in the flowers. Flowers that have been through this process are then cooked together with tea leaves. The most common scented tea—jasmine tea—is very popular in Beijing and Tianjin.

Nice Utensils for Tea

The fashion of drinking tea promotes the development of porcelain industry of China. Photo by Li Yuxiang.

Speaking of tea apparatus, they were inseparable from eating apparatus before Tang Dynasty. With the popularity of drinking tea, tea apparatus were getting more and more delicate. Lu Yu alone has mentioned over 20 kinds of apparatus and tools for tea picking, producing, containing, baking, cooking and drinking. The porcelain industry rapidly developed in Tang and Song dynasties under the fashion of drinking tea.

Take Tang people's tea bowl for example. There were various celadon with Yue kiln, Wuzhou kiln, Ou kiln and Yaozhou kiln as representatives, white porcelain represented by Xing kiln, and black porcelain famous for Deqing kiln. According to *Book of Tea*, "celadon is good for tea" while white, yellow and brown porcelain made the tea color red, purple and black respectively, none looking good. Celadon of Yue kiln was the best. The reason why porcelain from Xing kiln was less good than that from Yue kiln were enumerated in these three sentences: "Xing porcelain resembles silver while Yue porcelain is like jade," "Xing porcelain resembles snow while Yue porcelain is like ice," and "Xing porcelain is white and makes tea red while Yue porcelain is green and makes tea green." In the Chinese history of porcelain development, from Eastern Han when celadon was produced to Tang, among celadon kiln, Yue kiln developed fastest, had the most kiln spots, covered the largest area, and topped others in quality.

When it came to Song Dynasty, people preferred ordering tea and liked white tea soup. Also with the influence of tea contest, black-glaze porcelain was uplifted to the highest position. No famous kiln specialized in celadon or white porcelain but co-tempered black porcelain. The most praised in

A Jianyang ware porcelain bowl of Song Dynasty with the technique of "Rabbit Hair" from of Fujian.

historic literature was "Rabbit Hair" and "Oil Drop" from Jianyang kiln of Fujian. Those two kinds of black-glaze porcelain let out red from black, had thick porcelain fetus, and were good at heat preservation. Therefore they were the favorite for tea experts and they even once served in the imperial court, while celadon and white porcelain suffered from indifference.

In Ming Dynasty, with the catching on of drinking tea with loose leases, open apparatus were not only insufficient in giving off fragrance, but were inadequate in heat preservation, either. So teapot appeared with need. Cooking tea with small pots has now a history of 400 years since its introduction at the end of 16th century.

The producing place of purple-grit tea apparatus is Yixing—the famous "capital of porcelain" of China. It is located along Lake Tai, being a famous tea area as early as Tang Dynasty. Purple-grit tea apparatus of Yixing first appeared in late years of Tang. Coming to Ming, experts on making pots succeeded one after another, and purple-grit pot became the most fashionable and most valuable tea apparatus for its conformity with Ming people's pursuit of natural atmosphere when drinking tea. With good air permeability, purple-grit teapot not only keeps the original fragrance of tea leaves, but prevents it from getting the taste of ripe water. In winter purple-

A set of tea utensil of Qing Dynasty, including a tea pot with handle and four tea bowls.

Tiger-running Teahouse in Suzhou. Photo by Li Yuxiang.

grit teapot keeps the tea warm and in summer it prevents the tea from going sour. After long years of using, there will appear a layer of tea film on the inside wall of the pot, which can add to the sweetness of tea. Purple-grit teapot is delicate and lovely, exquisitely shaped and finely carved. People not only like using it for tea, but like caressing it as well. So the pot will obtain a purple sheen in the course of time. Lightly clouted, the pot gives a tiny sound of metals and stones. Purple-grit teapot is glazed in neither the inside nor the outside, so it has an antique look and gives a tinge of primitive and simple beauty. The pot body is decorated with carving and drawing, and the pot bottom is inscribed, too, combining calligraphy, painting, and sculpture in tea ceremony.

Therefore, purple-grit teapot has far exceeded its practical value.

Qing Dynasty saw the high development of porcelain and the rich variety of tea leaves. With different types of tea leaves, people had more choice of tea apparatus. In addition to the purple-grit pot of Yixing, color-glaze porcelain tea apparatus came up too, such as five-color, pink-color and enamel porcelain, which were graceful in shape and brilliant in color. The vast variety of tea apparatus brought people artistic enjoyment and pleasure when serving in tea drinking.

Tea-Zen Affinity

Tea is native Chinese plant while Buddhism is an imported religion. Originally they belonged to different groups but gradually became closely related, even inseparable from each other. People say tea-Zen affinity not without reason. Lu Yu said in his *The Book of Tea*, "tea is cold, most suitable for people in pursuit of morality and virtue." Tea tastes better in aftertaste, first bitter but sweet on careful savoring. This is secretly in accordance with the Buddhist aspiration for happiness after misery.

It is recorded in many spots in Lu Yu's *The Book of Tea* that as early as the time of Wei and Jin and Southern and Northern dynasties, monks attached great weight to tea and many famous temples in famous mountains planted tea of their own. The renowned monk Huiyuan of Eastern Jin (317–420) planted tea in Mount Lushan (in the north of Jiangxi Province in southeast China), and often drank tea and recited poems there all through the night. But it was not until Tang Dynasty that Buddhism exerted a really profound influence on Chinese tea culture. This had a lot to do with the generation of Zen Buddhism.

The India-originated Buddhism was introduced to China in Han Dynasty. After that, Buddhism and native Chinese ideologies like Confucianism and Taoism competed and merged, finally giving birth to a Buddhist sect with typical Chinese cultural traits—Zen Buddhism. Zen Buddhism was the crystallization of Buddhism assimilating Taoist thoughts. It could also be regarded as an alteration of Buddhism by ethics-valuing Confucianism. Yet Zen Buddhism still took Sakyamuni as its founder. Legend has it that Sakyamuni once picked a flower without saying a word. None of his disciples understood what that

Tea and Zen
Also called the 'Damo' school after Bodhidarma its founder, 'Chan' or 'Zen' (the meditation school) is one of the schools of Chinese Buddhism, and it gets its name because it sees meditation as the sum of Buddhist practice. The chief purpose of religious cultivation is seen as discerning one's original Buddha nature through meditation. The Chinese Chan school has a specially close connection with tea. The school began to flourish in the Early Tang period, and as it gained in popularity it became ever more common for Buddhists everywhere to sing the praises of tea-drinking. In the Middle Tang the monk Huaihai of Baizhang Mountain drew up the Baizhang monastic rule, and after that tea rituals in monasteries became ever more standard. In the pure tranquillity of their simple meditation halls it became everyday practice for Chan monks to offer tea to the Buddha, serve tea to guests, and to use tea to clear the mind and heart. For these monks tea-drinking ranked among the arts of 'chan' cultivation.

< The main gate to Huqiu Temple, Suzhou. Photo by Li Yuxiang.

meant except Mahagaya who smiled at his teacher. This anecdote illustrated Zen Buddhism's feature of "no words written, but understanding through spiritual communication."

Zen Buddhism maintains that everyone has Buddhist nature, so is capable of becoming Buddha. Nevertheless, according to different levels of practice, Zen Buddhism has two sects—the Sudden and the Gradual. People advocating gradual awakening believe human heart is originally pure but is polluted by prejudices and ambitions. What gymnosophists should do is to constantly remove their impurities, as they constantly dust a mirror. On the contrary, people advocating sudden awakening omit this drudgery of frequent cleaning, and insist that as long as one has a pure heart, one can become Buddha on the instant. In short, gradual awakening views the process of becoming Buddha as a change from impurity to purity, while sudden awakening basically denies the reality of pollution.

The sect of Gradual practices sitting Zen (sitting in meditation). Zen comes from Sanskrit, meaning heart cultivation and thought purification. While practicing, disciples sit with two legs put crosswise—left foot on right leg and right foot on left leg. Head is vertical and back straight, neither moving nor swaying, neither slanting nor leaning. Eyes look ahead or focus on one spot, to reach a state of calm meditation. As tea is able to have people stay fresh and awake, and will not cause overexcitement as strong wine, it is a requisite in this practice. According to legend, founder Dharma—who introduced Zen Buddhism to China—sliced off his eyelids to prevent sleep. From the flesh he threw on the ground generated tea trees. From this story we can get an idea of the affinity between tea and sitting Zen. Buddhism summarizes the good that tea does to sitting Zen in three points, knows as "Three Virtues." First, tea keeps people awake while sitting Zen at night. Second, it helps people digest while full. Last, it gives people a serene heart without desires. The earliest written record of sitting Zen started in East Jin, when a monk called Dan Daokai, in order to keep sleep away, took medicine every day and sometimes drank a special kind of tea called Tea Soda—a cooked combination of tea, ginger, laurel, orange, date, and other spices. Gradual's notion of changing from impurity to purity largely influenced the development of Chinese tea culture. It was in Tang Dynasty when Zen flourished that people wholly deserted the practice of adding condiments in tea. Lu Yu, who grew up in a temple, regarded the sticky and tasteless Tea Soda as "rubbish food." He wrote in a book, "put shallot, ginger, date, orange skin, dogwood, mint, etc. in a pot and cook them together... This is swill from drain." People started to pay attention to the natural pure and strong taste of tea, just like Zen advised people to seek and discover their own true and pure hearts.

Unlike the Gradual, the sect of Sudden almost completely abandoned the austerity of sitting Zen but replaced it with understanding Zen, whose most common practice was "understanding words," namely to dispel wrong ideas and achieve understanding through witty or even eccentric Qs and As. According to the sect of Sudden, Sudden realization was a practice for people innately gifted. That was to say, only fortunate and also intelligent people were likely to succeed in this practice, while those less gifted had better choose the sect of Gradual. However, because it was easier and funnier, sect of Sudden attracted more and more disciples and gradually took the lead among various sects of Buddhism. Many who practiced Gradual at first were converted into the Sudden. Daoyi (709–788) was one of them. This stubborn monk kept sitting Zen after following the Sudden. In order to illumine him, his master ground a brick in front of him. Daoyi asked his master why he did that. The master answered he was to make a mirror. Daoyi wondered, "How can a brick be ground to a mirror?" Master retorted, "If grinding brick doesn't make a mirror, how can sitting Zen make a Buddha?"

Although neglecting sitting Zen, sect of Sudden still took tea as a necessary complement in practicing. Having to "understand

Laughing Buddha at Lingyin Temple, Hangzhou. Photo by Li Yuxiang.

words," monks often gathered or traveled around, so tea drinking became necessary to add fun. Monks of the Sudden were equally fond of tea. Monk Zhaozhou of Tang Dynasty was a big fan. Whenever someone asked him to explain Zen or for advice, he answered them all with one sentence, "go and have tea!" At that time, tea, like basic daily necessities such as rice and oil, had permeated in the life of common people. People of all classes and in all positions were all in the habit of drinking tea. What Zhaozhou meant was that Zen was neither mysterious nor special, but was implied in daily life and common activities such as carrying water and drinking tea. As Master Huineng (638–713)—the inaugurator of sect of Sudden—said, "Buddhism is in the world and can be understood in the world. Seeking Buddhist wisdom elsewhere is like seeking rabbit's horn." Sect of Sudden gave as much favor and emphasis to tea as sect of Gradual, for the same reason that tea carried in it a spiritual correspondence with the sect. Sect of Sudden despised and even rejected language, which was similar to Taoism. A famous simile of the sect of Sudden goes like this: you can point where the moon is, but your finger is not equivalent to the moon. Likewise, language can only express truth but is not truth itself.

Zen transcends language, just as tea ceremony should give way to tea drinking. Zen generally resorts to intuitional experience and instantaneous realization, and went beyond manmade regulations and limitations. This was quite revolutionary at that time.

Zen not only affected the lower class, but was welcomed by rulers as well. Master Huineng was highly regarded by the female emperor Wu Zetian (624–705) and participated in making major policies. AD 849, an emperor of Tang Dynasty asked a 120-year-old monk for advices on longevity. The monk replied his longevity didn't depend on medicine but on tea. He drank 40 or 50 cups of tea every day, sometimes more than 100 cups. Although suppressing Buddhism once, Tang emperors were supportive and encouraging for Buddhism on the whole. Emperor Xizong (873–888) secretly hid golden and silver tea wares in the cellar of Famen Temple in Shaanxi Province, performing the highest royal rite. The fact that tea wares were carefully put together with the supreme treasure of Buddhism—Buddhist relic—in a special room was another convincing proof of the affinity between tea and Zen.

"Famous temples always produce good tea." Monks in Tang Dynasty were exempted from penal service and tax, so a lot of people became monks. Zen master Huaihai (meaning a heart as generous as sea) put forward the idea of "a day without work, a day without food," combining Zen understanding and labor to sparkplug a lifestyle of agriculture and Zen. Many temples had lands of their own and developed them into tea gardens to plant tea. A great many fame tea came from temples, called "Temple Tea." The well known Mengding tea is said to be planted by Zen master Puhui of Sweet Dew Temple (in Mount Mengshan in southwest China) with hands in Han Dynasty. It has been tribute tea from Jin Dynasty. Wuyi Rock tea from Wuyi Mountain of Fujian (in southeast China) is also best known for its "Longevity Eyebrow," "Lotus Heart" and "Phoenix Tail and Dragon Beard" produced in temples. In northern Song Dynasty, monks in Water & Moon Temple of Dongting Mount in Jiangsu Province (in east China) were very good at cooking tea. They made a kind of tea named after their temple—Water & Moon Tea, which became today's Pilochun. The celebrated poet Liu Yuxi (772–842) of Tang Dynasty mentioned in his poem that monks then invented a cultivating method of creating shade in the garden. They planted tea together with bamboo which could provide shade for tea trees and the tree absorbed the clear fragrance of bamboo. A monk picked leaves from these trees to treat guests. Fried in a pan, leaves filled the room with sweet smell. This was the earliest record of "frying green" method of cooking tea.

Poet and painter Zheng Banqiao (1693–1765) of Qing Dynasty wrote such a couplet: all personages like commenting on water, while all eminent monks love competing in tea. In temples, there were "tea monk" specialized in plating tea, "tea boss" in charge of cooking tea, and "tea-bestowing monk" responsible for bestowing tea. There were also "tea hall" and "tea room" where monks drank tea, read scripture, and discussed Zen principles. The hall of worship usually had drums. Those in the northeast corner were called "dharma drums" while those in the northwest corner were called "tea drums." Tea drum was wooden and hollow in the shape of a fish. Dharma drum was beaten during principle explanation and tea drum was beaten when monks gathered to drink tea. Tea was also served in the interlude between Zen sittings. Around every New Year, monks assembled to taste leaves planted by themselves. This was the famous ceremony of "Popularizing Tea." Jingshan Temple in Mount Tianmu of Zhejiang Province—known as the best Zen temple to the south of Yangtze River—held a tea party every spring, in which the chief master cooked tea in person and tea monks served tea to monks and guests present. Taking tea, monks and guests smelt its savor, observed its color, tasted its flavor, and graded its quality. This kind of tea party lasted over 100 years from Song Dynasty to Yuan Dynasty. Other similar tea meetings and tea parties also existed. Those in consecration to Buddha were "Memorial Tea." Those sipped according to

Meditation Tearoom. Photo by Li Yuxiang.

the length of monkhood were "Abnegation Tea." Those serving only tea were "Tea Meeting." Some temples bathed the figures of Buddha with tea, called "Buddha Washing Tea." Men of letters took part in these tea meetings, too. So they and monks gave tea leaves to each other, or they treated friends with tea, promoting tea drinking to be a widespread fashion. In Southern Song Dynasty (1127–1279), temple often held large-scale tea parties that could contain more than 1,000 people. Stipulations about tea drinking have been drawn out and became part of Buddhist principles.

Famous Zen masters were usually experts on tea. Lu Yu's good friend Jiaoran—a poet and a monk—was the first one to put forward the phrase "tea ceremony." Some even took him as the inaugurator of tea ceremony. Among his many poems about tea, one was *Ode to Tea Drinking*, in which he wrote:

One sip dispels sleepiness and thoughts got clear and active;

Second sip refreshes my mind like fine raindrops descending on dust;

Third sip brings enlightenment and worries evaporated without much ado.

If we compare the level of tea drinking with the process of virtue cultivation, a lot of Zen masters' skill in cooking and valuing tea reached a superb state. Monk Zhiji, who raised Lu Yu, was used to drinking tea cooked by Lu Yu and stopped drinking tea after Lu Yu left. Hearing of this, the emperor invited him over and asked

him to drink the tea cooked by several tea masters. But the monk put down every cup after one sip. Only when the emperor asked Lu Yu to secretly bring his tea that Zhiji exclaimed, "This is the tea cooked by Lu Yu!" Another story was even more incredible. In Song Dynasty, experienced tea masters created ripples in a cup while cooking tea. These ripples took on various forms—mountains, sun and moon, birds and beasts, etc., so it was called "Tea Opera" or "Water Painting." A top Zen master could come up with a poetic sentence out of the ripples of every cup, and four cups gave him an elegant Jueju, a traditional Chinese poetic form of four lines with a strict rhyme scheme.

A kind of new tea called Taiping Houkui. Photo by Li Yuxiang.

The importance of tea to Buddhism was not just in the sect of Zen. Sect of Mi in Tang Dynasty also considered tea as the best offerings for Buddha. What was more, in its circulation, Chinese tea culture went abroad to Japan. In AD 803, a Japanese monk Saichou came to China to study Buddhist knowledge. When he returned to Japan two years later after finishing studying, he took tea seeds of Mount Tiantai (in Zhejiang Province in east China) with him, bringing Japanese history without tea to an end. Saichou sowed the seeds in Hiyoshijinja of Hieizani in Kyoto. Even today Hiyoshijinja had an epitaph like this: "This is the earliest tea garden of Japan." In Southern Song Dynasty, a Japanese monk Eisai also came to China in pursuit of Buddhism. After going back, he wrote the first book on tea in Japan—*Keeping Health with Tea*. Eisai thought that medicine only cured one disease while tea cured all diseases. He also recorded the ways of making and drinking tea in Southern Song Dynasty, and was esteemed as "found of tea in Japan." About the time of Ming Dynasty, based on the literature left

< The tea of Taipinghoukui is from the remote mountains of Anhui Province. Photo by Li Yuxiang.

by these Tang-visiting monks, Qian Lixiu founded Japanese tea ceremony featured in "harmony, respect, serenity, and quietness." Though not a monk, Qian Lixiu fully comprehended the essential affinity between Zen and tea. He said, "the essence of tea is no other than boiling water and cooking tea." This concept of "Zen in life" is in perfect agreement with what Zhaozhou monk and Master Huineng once said.

Tea Ceremony in China

The Chinese love drinking tea. They drink tea to relieve thirst when thirsty, to sober up when drunken, to help digest after a meal, and to stay awake and fresh when staying up at night. Men of literature and writing take tea not only as a material enjoyment, but also as a spiritual pleasure. They refine the ceremony of tea drinking and are particular about water, apparatus, occasion, time, and people that are involved in tea drinking. This activity summarizes the essence of Chinese culture and implies the affection and pursuit of Chinese people.

Good tea requires good water, because only in that way can tea have good taste, so tea lovers from ancient time to the present have always taken water as a key point in tea drinking. "Water of Yangtze River and tea of Mount Mengshan top" has been said for thousands of years. The world-known tiger-running spring of Hangzhou of Zhejiang Province can best match Longjing tea. Lu Yu wrote in his *The Book of Tea* that "water in mountains is best, in rivers is ok, and in wells is second rate." Water is valuable for being the active water at the source of rivers. Lu Yu held that mountain water that flowed from white rock cracks was the best while spouting or dropping water usually caused diseases in people's necks. The stale water in valleys was inedible but river water from those less inhabited sections was better because it was less polluted. Well water from the deep wells with waves was preferred. Lu Yu even divided the water of all China into 20 grades. Liu Bochu—another man of letters—chose the Nanling water of Yangtze river as the best in the world and the well water from Huishan Mount of Wuxi, Jiangsu as the second best. Nanling water was situated in the vicinities of Jinshan, Jiangsu. Only the water fetched in copper bottles tied to long ropes

The Dao of Tea

The 'dao' of tea in broad terms refers to the arts of making and drinking tea; it is both one of the rituals of life, with tea as its medium, and a mode of self-cultivation. Through brewing tea, appreciating its appearance, savouring its fragrance and relishing its taste, peace comes to the heart and strength to one's moral nature, and one's feelings and conduct are reshaped. The 'dao' of tea in China flourished under the Tang, and its practitioners were very particular about the quality of five conditions: the tea leaves, the water, the heating time and temperature, the tea vessels, and the surroundings. At the same time they matched the occasion to such other conditions as mood, seeking perfect harmony between the external flavour of the tea and the inner world of the heart.

< The elegant tea room and gentle music take people's mind into a tranquil world. Photo by Li Yuxiang.

III

from deep down the water from 0 a.m. to 2 a.m. and from 12 a.m. to 2 p.m. could be called Nanling water. Since it was so hard to get, the second best—Huishan Mount well water—became the coveted target of all. Chancellor Li Deyu of Tang Dynasty used his power to establish a special water-passing organization, just in order to have constant access to Huishan Mount well water. The well water would be transported all the way from Wuxi to Xi'an for his enjoyment. The Song Dynasty still held Huishan Mount well water in a high position. To keep the freshness of water during the long journey, Song people invented fresh-keeping methods like sprinkling through fine sand and impurity-ridding. In Ming Dynasty, it was common to put white stones in water to better water's quality.

The purple-grit tea pot made by Chen Mingyuan, a famous ceramist of Qing Dynasty.

Drinking apparatus are another important part of Chinese tea ceremony. Different times have different sets of tea apparatus in fashion. Lu Yu, in his *The Book of Tea*, recorded 24 kinds of apparatus and making methods, including wind stove for frying water, clips for clipping coal, bamboo clips for stirring water, etc. Tea apparatus can not only fully exhibit the fragrance of tea, but its visual aesthetic beauty as well. Lu Yu held that the color of white, yellow and brown were not suitable for tea apparatus because they were too similar to the color of tea. This is for the same reason why we use glasses to drink green tea, with a view of observing the floating and sinking of leaves in the glass.

Chinese tea ceremony also has stipulations as to the time and locations of tea drinking. Since tea tree is "good wood of the south," tea is also considered as the result of integrating the marrow of sky, earth, and nature. The hills, mist, bright moon and cool breeze

Warming up the tea utensils before tasting Kungfu Tea. Photo by Li Yuxiang.

bring about the special characters and appearances of tea. That's why the Chinese emphasize the harmony between humans and nature in tea drinking. *Cha Shu* (rough remarks on tea) of Ming Dynasty has made detailed definitions as to what time, location and environment is or is not good for tea drinking. For example, it is good to drink tea when you are in leisure time, but not so when you are busy, as you don't have time to fully appreciate it, which is a waste of good tea. It is also good to drink tea on moderately sunny or rainy days, on bridges or boats, in forests or among high and straight bamboos, in shaded pavilions surrounded by lotus, or in a little censed yard, while damp room, kitchens, public streets and places with many children playing and crying are not suitable for tea drinking. Another book *Analysis of Tea* also mentioned that if you cook tea at night in remote mountains, the mixture of the sound of water boiling inside and of pines whispering outside and the vague tea fragrance flowing in the room combine to create an atmosphere where both the inner world of human heart and outer world of nature are forgotten. In short, tea drinking should avoid boisterous and untidy occasions. That's why it's fit to drink tea while listening to melody but not while watching opera, because melody seems remote and relaxing, whereas opera is too clamorous.

Tea tastes thin and distant, embodying a spiritual state of serenity and indifference to fame and fortune, and epitomizing the Chinese social philosophy of "remaining tranquil in favor or humiliation" and "contentment brings happiness." Unlike wine drinking, which demands a lot of people to show excitement, tea drinking exactly needs to avoid excitement. Ancient people believed that it was better to involve few people when drinking tea, because as long as there was communication with nature, even drinking alone can be cheerful. Drinking tea alone accentuates spiritual comprehension and enjoyment, for "being content with poverty and keen on morality" is the utmost spirit of tea. Drinking tea with another accentuates fun, for to appreciate tea with good

Putting some oolong tea gently into a purple-grit tea pot. Photo by Li Yuxiang.

friends at night is the best illustration of the old saying —friendship between noble figures is pure like water. Drinking tea among three people accentuates taste. The Chinese character for "taste" is "品," which is a combination of three "口," meaning mouth. It vividly symbolizes the scene of three people sitting around a stove. "One person drinking means serenity; two means goodness, three or four means fun, five or six means generality, and seven or eight means charity." The noise occasion of two many human voices will strip tea drinking of its elegant charm and vitality.

The purple-grit tea pot made by Yang Pengnian, a famous ceramist of Qing Dynasty.

Chinese tea culture reached its height of fame and splendor in Song Dynasty, and tea ceremony also climbed to its peak at that time. From emperor and ministers to common citizens, almost everyone had the habit of drinking tea. There even appeared a "Contest of Tea" for people to compete in their skills of making tea.

Contest of tea is also known as War of *Ming*, which

stemmed from Tang Dynasty. At that time Jianzhou of Fujian Province was a famous tea area producing tribute tea. When new leaves came out, local tea farmers would gather together to grade the leaves and compete in their tea cooking skills. Contestants, lookers-on, and evaluators were all there. It was like a major sport event. In Song Dynasty, contest of tea became popular all over the country. Even rulers and men of letters participated in it, like Su Shi and Cai Xiang, the contest between whom has been told by many. In the contest, Cai Xiang brought high-quality tea and chose the well known Huishan Mount well water. He was expected to win. But to everyone's surprise, Su Shi used water boiled in burned bamboo (a kind of Chinese traditional medicine) and won the contest at last. That has been a household story for quite a while.

Pouring boiling water into tea pot, heating tea leaves evenly. Photo by Li Yuxiang.

The contest of tea emphasized three points: tea leaves, water, and apparatus. The leaves should be picked in the same year, with Dragon & Phoenix Cake being the most precious. Spring water, rain or snow was preferred. As to apparatus, black porcelain from Jianzhou of Fujian Province was best known. The contest was pretty complex. First, warm the cups; then start boiling water which was also called "soup waiting." Song people usually used tea vase to boil water, so they could not observe the "Three Boil" process in Fu as Tang people did. They could only rely on their listening ability. Books about tea of Song Dynasty recorded the ways of differentiating water by their sound. If the water in vase sounded like cicada or insect singing, it was "First Boil." If it sounded like cars driving in a distance, it was "Second Boil." When it sounded like pines waving in the wind, "Three Boil"

was achieved. Tea cakes should be first pounded to pieces and then ground, the smaller the pieces, the better. Leaf pieces should be cooked immediately after grinding without delay. Song people drank the tea water and ate the leaves, which was different from what we do today. Because of that, the water temperature became extremely important. If the temperature was too low, the pieces would float on the water surface; if it was too high, they would sink to the bottom. Both of these two situations should be avoided, and people therefore said "soup waiting" was most difficult. Some claimed that water should be put aside for a while after boiling, to wait for the right temperature for tea cooking.

Afterwards, put the triturated tea powder in cups, add little boiling water and mix them into paste. This was called "paste making." Then came the step of "Diantang" (water adding). Pour water from vase into cup. The wrist holding the vase should turn deftly while pouring, so that water would burst out like a stable water spout, which couldn't be off and on or thick at one time and thin at another but should be even and straight. When the cup was about 60% full of water, stop pouring. The water spout, too, had to stop suddenly without any loose drops. When "Diantang" was going on, "Jifu" (incessantly stir water with tea chopstick) was performed at the same time to produce pure white froth in the cup. While stirring, fingers were brought to move by wrist at an even speed and with even power, otherwise you couldn't attain the best effect. The simultaneous performance of "Diantang" and "Jifu" required excellent cooperation of both hands. Any carelessness or neglect might result in losing the contest. *General Remarks on Tea* by Emperor Huizong of Song Dynasty divided the contest into seven phases from paste making to Diantang and Jifu, each phase involving different techniques.

How did people decide the result of the contest? The first step was to observe the color of tea water and to compare the froth. Since tea cake lost its juice during the process, the tea took on a whitish color. Pure white indicated that leaves were fresh and tender and finely processed, so it was the best choice. In contrast, darkish color of the tea water suggested that the step of steaming green wasn't thoroughly done, yellowish color pointed out old leaves, and reddish color showed over-baking. All of these colors

Distributing the first-round tea soup into fragrance-appreciating cups circularly. Photo by Li Yuxiang.

indicated low quality of tea. The evaluation of froth was even more demanding. Froth should be even, tiny and dense, like a few stars around a brilliant moon, or even taking on the shapes of birds, beasts, insects or fish. Froth was not supposed to disappear quickly, but should last a long time and stick to the sides of the cup. When froth dispersed, it left water trail on the cup wall. People then decided who won or who lost by whether the water trail appeared early or late. The later it came, the more likely it was to win. Since Song people attached so much importance to the white purity of water's color and the duration of froth, tea apparatus came to be a decisive factor in winning or losing the contest of tea. The best loved apparatus was the black-glazed rabbit-hair cup made in Jian kiln of Fujian. This cup received such a warm welcome because its oily blackness well foiled the whiteness of water, and its rabbit-hair-like veins on the inside wall kept the froth from dispersing. Also for the sake of the contest of tea, Song people took rare tea trees with white leaves as a peerless treasure.

Tasting with tongue was after observing with eyes. The taste was considered better if it included four characters—fragrant, sweet, heavy, and smooth. The smell was deemed better if it permeated quickly once the tea got in the cup. The winner could only be decided after a comprehensive evaluation.

With the complete substitution of loose tea for roll tea and cake tea, the once flourishing fashion of contest of tea in Song Dynasty died out, and Chinese tea ceremony took up various forms. Today, Kungfu tea, which is popular in Fujian, Guangdong, Taiwan and other places, is a representative of Chinese tea ceremony.

Kungfu means sophisticated and adept skills. Since Qing Dynasty, Kungfu tea has had its fixed formalities. The best apparatus for Kungfu tea is purple-grit pottery. The pot is as tiny as a fist, and the cup is just the size of half a table tennis ball. The apparatus are made small so that once the tea is made, you can finish it immediately, thus preserving the fresh taste of tea. The cooking-enduring oolong tea is normally cooked as Kungfu tea. Before cooking, pot and cup are washed with hot water to raise their temperature. Then leaves are added to about 70% or 80% full, so that the teapot is just full after water is poured in. After that boiling water is poured in from high. This first round is not to be drunk but thrown away at once. The purpose of it is to wash tea—to clear the leaves of the dust and impurities on them. Later boiling water

Guan Gong Patrolling the Defense

Guan Gong, or Guan Yu (160?–220), is a famous general of the Shu and Han (221–263) Reign of the Three Kingdoms Period (220–280). "Patrolling the city" refers to a military commander inspecting the fortification, armaments and morale of the army. When Guan Gong is patrolling, he attends to each and every detail. So in a tea ceremony, the allusion means that one pours tea in each cup.

Distributing the rest tea soup to each cup evenly, showing respect to each guest. Photo by Li Yuxiang.

(Top) Pouring the first-round tea soup on the tea pot to "nourish" it. Photo by Li Yuxiang. >
(Bottom) Covering the fragrance-smelling cups with tea-drinking cups. Photo by Li Yuxiang.

Pouring the second-round tea soup in fragrance-smelling cups into tea-drinking cups. Photo by Li Yuxiang.

is added again until it overflows the pot. Remove the floating froth with pot lid, put on the lid, and drench the whole pot with boiling water. On the one hand, this can rid the pot of the remaining froth. On the other hand, it can raise the pot's temperature and send forth the tea fragrance quicker. In about a minute, this second round can be tasted. When you fill the cup, the pot should be held at a low height to keep the water temperature as well as prevent froth. The way of pouring Kungfu tea is very unusual. All cups are put together and the pot is moved quickly from one cup to another without stop. This is called "Guangong (a great general at the time of Three Kingdoms in Chinese history) Inspecting the City." Its aim is to make every cup of tea have the same even taste, thus showing equal respect to each person. When the pot is about empty, the remnant tea will be dropped into each cup evenly. With the last cup, the water is just over. This is called "Han Xin (a great army officer at Guangong's time) Roll-calling Troops." The last

Strong fragrance lingering in the fragrance-smelling cups. Photo by Li Yuxiang.

Take the tea-drinking cup, smell the fragrance first, and then tasting the tea. Photo by Li Yuxiang.

step is to taste. First the color is observed. Second the fragrance is smelt. Last the tea is tasted. While tasting, tea is retained in mouth and the tongue turns within to fully feel its profundity. After all these steps, tea is swallowed slowly. The worst thing is to wolf it all down in one mouthful, which totally spoils the mood and atmosphere.

Han Xin Mustering the Troops
Han Xin (?–196 B.C.) is a famous general of the founding of state in the Western Han Dynasty. "Mustering the Troops" refers to the military commander reviewing the troops, counting the number of soldiers and raising the morale of the army before going out for the battle. When Han Xin is "mustering the troops", the more soldiers, the better. So in a tea ceremony, this allusion means that it is always preferable to share more essence of the tea soup.

A purple-grit tea pot of Qing Dynasty covered with colorful enamel.

Tea-drinking Customs

Tea ceremonies are not mystic. They are both commonplace and elevated, just like the character of Chinese people, casual and natural, not restricted by certain patterns. Provided by Huang Rui.

A Chinese proverb goes like this—the first seven things a day are firewood, rice, oil, salt, catsup, vinegar and tea. Tea is an indispensable part in the life of Chinese people. The first six of the seven things are used either as fuel or condiment for cooking, having something to do with feeding people. Tea is the only drink. Although it ranks last in the first seven things, it occupies a special position.

For the Chinese, tea is far more than just a kind of drink. The spirit and verve of tea is deeply branded in the national character of the Chinese people. When we look back to the developing journey of Chinese nation, we discover that, since the time of Shen Nong, every historical phase reflects the impact of tea; every ideological trend renovates the connotation of tea; every regional group has its specific understanding of tea; and every detail in life is wrapped with the thin aroma of tea. From picking, making, cooking to drinking, every step conveys profound cultural implication. The Chinese discover and make tea, and tea slowly changes the life of the Chinese.

Stemming from remote mountains, tea absorbs the essence of natural molding. Going through manual work, tea condenses human intelligence and talent. Tea, in which nature and nurture co-exist in harmony and simplicity and sophistication combine in perfection, best symbolizes the unique Chinese culture of "integration of nature and man."

Confucius—founder of Confucianism who lived more than 2,000 years ago—said, "the bygone is like this, day and night without stop," regretting that time was like flowing water, endlessly going ahead. A Chinese folksay also has it, "a piece of time is like a piece of gold, but this piece of gold is not enough to buy this piece of time." Ancient Chinese accentuated the value of time and advised people to seize every chance because lost chance never came back. This is well reflected in tea picking. Time plays an essential role in tea picking. Picked several days earlier, the leaves are peerless treasures. But if picked several days later, they are no better than

Tea drinking is just people's habit in everyday life. Photo by Li Yuxiang.

common. What tea-picking requires is accurate grasp of chance.

Fame teas are mostly from famous mountains. Since "water and soil in a certain place raise certain kind of people," the development of humans is closely bound up with natural environment. Northern people are generous and straightforward while southern people are reserved and mild. Tea leaves produced from different regions also take on strong local characteristics, in response to the characteristics of local people.

Lu Yu said that good tea leaves didn't rely on producing places and that making techniques were the real key factor to decide the quality of tea leaves. Tea leaves should be deprived of their "green," like crude jade should be carved and refined. People also became tranquil and philosophical after a life of tempering. The ancients believed in "similar in nature but far apart in culture," saying that the power that shaped our personality and quality was postnatal experience and effort.

Tea frying demands the right degree of heating. Tea cooking asks for the right water temperature. The Chinese stress the right degree in everything. "For those walking 100 Li (a Chinese measurement in length about 500 meters), 90 Li is only half the distance." If tea is not heated enough or water isn't hot enough, tea fragrance can't be fully exerted. "Better lack than shoddiness." "Excess is worse than inadequacy." If tea is heated too much or water is too hot, the original taste of tea will be spoiled and thus affecting the taste of tea.

While cooking tea, water should be absolutely clean and apparatus should be repeatedly washed as well. This is in accordance with Confucius' theory of "three times of self-reflection a day," unremittingly striving for moral purification.

Tea ceremony, which agglomerates the marrow of Chinese culture, is not a complicated ritual but an enjoyment pleasant to both body and mind. All Chinese people, male and female, old and young, have a special affection for tea. Various kinds of tea can respond to various phases of life.

In adolescence, people are like green tea, immature and simple. They don't know much but start to understand. They are still natural and this naturalness is displayed in every movement. Although not so strong in flavor, they are pure and lovely upon careful savoring.

In youth, people are like flower tea, in their flowery years with flowery scent and flowery dreams. Countless possibilities are in store for them. Whatever we add in the tea—jasmine, sweet-scented osmanthus or rose, this cup of tea is always redolent, admirable and appealing.

In middle age, people are like black tea, salmon in color and full of aroma. They are not as clear and fresh as green tea, but they have a mature charm of their own.

In old age, people are like Pu'er Tea, the older the better. Filled with all kinds of stories, elder people minutely represent traces of age. Though dry, old and thin in appearances, they are very intense and mellow in taste, able to stand up to repeated appreciation.

Tea utensils made of pottery. Photo by Xie Guanghui, Provided by *China Tourism*, Hong Kong.

The farmers of Lahu Nationality in Xishuangbanna, Yunnan province, are picking up spring tea.
Photo by Li Zhisen, provided by *China Tourism*, Hong Kong.

Tea with Friends

Western people are accustomed to treating guests with coffee while Chinese people prefer tea. "Present tea as wine to a guest arriving on a cold night while water is boiling in the bamboo stove on reddening fire." Host presents a cup of fragrant tea to show his hospitality. Generally, apparatus for guests to drink tea should be clean, and the rule of "tea 50% full and wine 100% full" should be observed when serving tea. Because hot tea tastes better, and it will get cooler if the guest cannot finish a full cup of tea. When there is only 1/3 of water left in the cup, host should re-fill the cup. As tea can help people digest, it is bad for the stomach if one drinks it with an empty belly. So when treating guests with tea, host usually serves some delicious snacks as accompaniment.

Because of the differences in grade, quality and price of tea leaves, the Chinese usually keep the best leaves for good friends or honored guests. According to legend, the poet of Song Dynasty—Su Shi—once visited the chief monk of a temple. At first, the chief monk didn't know who Su Shi was and didn't take him seriously, simply asking him to sit. Talking for a while, he found out that Su Shi was not a common man, so he said "pleas take a seat" and asked his monks to "bring tea." At last he realized the man in front of him was the celebrated Sir Dong Po. The chief monk deeply regretted his not knowing better and repeated, "Please take a good seat" and ordered his men to "bring good tea." What kind of tea the host serves the guest well illustrates what kind of position the guest takes in the eyes of the host. When Mr. Nixon—the president of America—visited China in 1972, Prime Minister Zhou Enlai personally invited him to Hangzhou—the heaven on earth—to have a taste of the typical Chinese good tea—West Lake Longjing.

To treat guests with tea is not a custom confined to Han nationality. Ethnic groups do so, too. For the Bai nationality of Yunnan, the most respectful way of treating a guest is to serve "Three-Course Tea," which has a parlance of "firstly bitter, secondly sweet, and lastly aftertaste," implying the vicissitude of life. When honored guest arrives, the hospitable Bai people lead him in to sit in front of a fire. After the water boils, host takes out the special grit jar for tea making, puts it on the fire, and adds leaves into it. Host will shake the jar to evenly warm the leaves, and add boiling water later. When the water enters the heated grit jar, the steam will make an enormous thunder-like sound. So this tea is also called "Thunder-sound Tea." When the tea is ready, it is served to each guest. This is the first course—bitter tea. The first course has the color of amber and tastes bitter and acerbic, but leaves a mouthful of after fragrance, totally dispelling the journey exhaustion. Right after this the second course is presented. Based on the first course, it has brown sugar, honey, walnut powder, pine nut, and other condiments, so it is called "sweet course," tasting sweet and mellow. The last course—"aftertaste course" contains even more condiments such as ginger, Chinese prickly ash, cassia bark, sesame, peanut powder, etc., tasting peppery and hot. In the language of Bai nationality, the sound for "peppery" is the same as that of "rich," "hot," and "intimate." The peppery and hot third course is to show that host treats the guest as relative. Meanwhile, it expresses the good wish to get rich as soon as possible. When drinking "aftertaste course," Bai people invite guests to dance. Both host and guest sing and dance together, enjoying themselves to their hearts' content. The leaves, cups and plates for "Three-Course Tea" are all specially made, and the decorum of serving tea involves 18 steps. Each course is served by two girls or boys, one of whom holds the plate and the other takes a "tea serving" bow to the guest first and then holds the cup with both hands to the height of his or her eyebrows, to show his or her respect for the guest.

Tea is not only to show welcome but refusal as well. In the world of officials in Qing Dynasty, there was a custom of "serving tea and showing the door." When a guest came to an official's home, he was generally treated with tea. But tea drinking was different from wine drinking. Host might persuade guests to take tea, but he wouldn't raise the cup for a toast like in wine drinking. If the host didn't like the visitor, or he had urgent affairs in hand, he would raise his own cup and asked the visitor to drink, hoping that he would leave as soon as the tea was finished. The guest normally understood and took his leave, without actually drinking up the tea.

Tea and Marriage

In chapter 25 of *Red Mansion Dream*, Wang Xifeng sends Lin Daiyu two bottles of tea leaves and joked, "You've drunk the tea of our family, how come you are still not the daughter-in-law of our family?" What brought tea and marriage together?

Tea ceremony is still kept in marriage custom in many tea-planting areas of China. Photo by Li Yuxiang.

Ancient Chinese considered marriage as the origin of all ceremonies. *Zhou Yi*—the classic book of Confucianism—said, "sky and earth give birth to all beings, all beings give rise to couples, couples give rise to fathers and sons, fathers and sons give rise to kings and ministers, kings and ministers give rise to the order of high and low, and high and low give rise to mistakes in ceremony." Marriage is regarded as the footstone of the entire moral system, so the durability and stability of marriage has been considerably stressed, as is said in "the principle of marriage is eternity as opposed to ephemerality." From courtship to wedding, certain rules and formalities have to be observed and certain gifts have to be presented. This not only shows respect to marriage, but implies people's good wish to the future married life.

In ancient China, a boy going to a girl's family had to bring a wild goose as gift, called "goose foundation." Wild goose is migratory bird that

"San Dao Cha" tea ceremony is the highest ceremony to treat guests as far as the people of Bai Nationality in Yunnan. Provided by *China Tourism*, Hong Kong.

migrates to the south in winter, so ancient people took them as "sun bird." The Chinese character for sun is called *Yang*. Since men belong to *Yang*, they expect their future wives to follow them as wild goose following sun. This obedience is called "husband sings and wife follows," suggesting a perfect domestic harmony. Besides, wild goose is loyal. It doesn't live on alone after its partner dies. People expect couples to be that loyal too and can live and die together. Later, it gets harder and harder to catch wild goose, so people substitute them with home-raised chicken, duck, and goose. With the popularization of tea, it superseded these poultries to be the best gifts for proposing. In a very long time, Chinese people planted tea trees by sowing seeds because they thought tea trees could not be transplanted for fear of dying of drying up. Ancient people expressed through tea their nice wish that their daughter would take root in her husband's family and be loyal all her life, just like a tea tree. If a woman re-married, that was "drinking the tea of two families." That woman was sure to be despised.

In Tang Dynasty, custom went so that tea was treated as betrothal gift. Since Song Dynasty, tea was even more closely related to wedding. Betrothal gift was also "tea gift," and to present betrothal gift was commonly called to "present tea." If a girl accepted the gift, that was "drink tea." To return the gift, fruits were usually chosen, sometimes together with tea, called "order tea." Even today, in the countryside in many parts of China, engagement is still called "accept tea" and the cash gift in engagement is called "tea cash." If both the boy and girl were willing, they appointed a time to get married. Many guests were invited to attend the wedding, during which tea, wine, music and opera were four necessary ingredients. In Qing Dynasty, the wedding ceremony developed to the systemized ceremony of "Three Tea," namely "present tea" when proposing, "settle tea" in wedding, and "join tea" on the first night of marriage. According to Lu You's *Notes from Hut of Old Knowledge*, in some southern regions at Lu You's time, single boys and girls got together to sing. Boys started with a song with "girls are flowers, come for tea sometimes." So tea was a good excuse for a date. In Hunan Province of mid-south China, tea was also the best tool for boys and girls to communicate. When a boy went to a girl's home on a blind date, the girl would serve him tea in person if she was satisfied with him. And the boy would accept the tea if he was also satisfied. The story didn't stop at this. Match making, blind date and bridal night were all accompanied by tea to add some fun. The custom of using tea as a matchmaker was not limited among common folks, either. It even influenced the aristocrats. When a royal man got married in Song Dynasty, he had to present 50 kilos of tea leaves as betrothal gift. The connection between tea and marriage was so intimate that it's almost "no marriage without tea." Emperor Kangxi

(1654–1722) of Qing Dynasty used to send ministers to south China (south of Yangtze river) to choose wives for him. Girls there all hurried to get married to avoid the widow-like life in the imperial palace. Nevertheless, however poor they the boys were and however hurried they were, tea was by no means dispensable.

Even after marriage, tea could not be done without. It played a role of stabilizing family and promoting conjugal emotion. In Ningbo of Zhejiang Province, there was a custom of "tea of new son-in-law." When the son-in-law went to his wife's home for the first time after marriage, his parents-in-law would lavishly entertain him with many dishes. Moderate family generally presented tea two or three times, and rich family could present as many as seven or eight times. The girl's family put their expectation for the son-in-law in the tea. Local people believed that even though discords occurred between the couple, as long as the husband remembered how well his parents-in-law once treated him, he would treat his wife kindly.

Not only did people associate the planting of tea trees with loyalty, but poets of past time liked to compare tea to girls as well. Su Shi had a sentence "good tea is always like beautiful woman." Poet Chen Yuyi of Song Dynasty also wrote a sentence "your black skirt and beautiful face look familiar and camellia blooms are all around in September." Because of tea's symbolic as well as practical value in the married life of Chinese people, it has been given enormous recognition and praise. In old China, when you went to another house as a guest, you could not bring tea leaves as gift if the host had a single daughter, because that would cause misunderstanding. However, now the Chinese don't need "order of parents and words of matchmaker," but prefer free love, so this function of tea has gradually gone to oblivion.

< A young girl of Bai Nationality is cooking tea. Photo by Xie Guanghui, provided by *China Tourism*, Hong Kong.

The boiling water pouring from a high point can cool down slightly so as to warm the tea leaves perfectly. Provided by Huang Rui.

Interesting Tea Drinking Customs

China has a vast territory. Over the centuries, a wide variety of tea drinking methods have emerged in different regions. Traditionally, the Hakka people in Hunan, Jiangxi, Fujian and Guangdong have enjoyed "mashed tea", and the skills of tea mashing are even regarded as a yardstick of the competence of a housewife. Hakka girls who don't know how to mash tea will have a lot of trouble finding their Mr. Right.

A typical Hakka household is armed with a set of devices for mashing tea: a pottery mortar, a wooden pestle, and a bamboo sieve for filtering out dregs. Tea leaves, soybeans, peanuts, corn, sesames and gingers are placed in the mortar and mixed with a small amount of cool boiled water. These ingredients are then crushed with the pestle, and the bamboo sieve is used to filter out the dregs, resulting in a "mashed mixture" like syeast or fruit concentrate. The "mashed mixture" is kept in a pottery jar. A few scoops of the mixture infused in boiling water will make a cup of mashed tea which will leave a long aftertaste and lingering aroma.

Heating Flower-and-Grass tea. Provided by Huang Rui.

Guangdong people are famous for their passion for "morning tea". Despite its name, the morning tea is not necessarily consumed in the morning. It can begin in the early morning and last until two or three o'clock in the afternoon. Teahouses typically offer a wide array of teas, such as oolong tea, green tea, black tea, and flower tea, for customers to choose from. They also provide a varied range of small dishes for the tea, such as roast pork buns, shrimp dumplings, pork and mushroom dumplings, and wontons. Morning tea customers often chat with each other or read newspapers while sipping the tea and nibbling on the snacks. Morning tea occasions give people the opportunity to socialize and enjoy one another's company.

Sichuan is the birthplace of Chinese tea and the cradle of the Chinese tea culture. Streets in cities around Sichuan are lined by teahouses of every description. Sichuan people are fond of "bowl tea". A ceramic set of bowls, consisting of a "tea vessel", a tea cover, and a tea bowl, is typically used. The "tea vessel" holds the tea bowl for insulation purposes. The tea cover is perhaps the greatest invention of Sichuan people in tea tasting. It serves various purposes. It can be placed on top of the tea bowl to form a tight space in which the flavor of the tea leaves can be extracted at a faster rate. It can also be used to scrape off the tea leaves floating on the top of the bowl. People who cannot wait to savor the tea can simply pour the hot tea onto the overturned tea cover so that it will cool down faster. A customer may also place the tea cover upside down on the bowl as a gesture for the waiter to get a refill. Sichuan people believe that the water boiled by iron ware or aluminum ware may undermine the flavor of the tea, and therefore they usually boil water in copper kettle with a long nozzle. Tea is poured from the copper kettle by a skilled waiter. He just aims the nozzle of the kettle at the bowl and raises his arm, and the water will shoot into the bowl. As the water fills to the brim, he will just lower his elbow, and the water shooting will immediately stop without spilling a drop. The bowl is then covered, ready to serve.

Tibetans don't infuse tea; they decoct it with salt in the way of the people of the Tang Dynasty in Lu Yu's time. A Tibetan saying goes, "Tea without salt is as tasteless as water; a man without money is as terrible as a ghost." Tibetans not only add salt to tea; they also put other ingredients in their tea. Tibetans are particularly fond of buttered tea. Most Tibetan households keep a special bucket for preparing buttered tea. They pour water-decocted tea leaves into the bucket and add butter, salt, egg, and walnut kernels. They then vigorously press and stir the mixture with a wooden stick whose lower end is fitted with a round disc unless the tea soup and the butter are fully integrated, resulting in a buttered tea which will leave a pleasant lingering taste. Tibetans, who live in high-altitude frigid regions, drink buttered tea to fend off cold, replenish their energy and prevent chapped lips, and therefore the buttered tea is immensely popular among the Tibetans.

Elegance in tea cup

Men of letters in the past all had indissoluble relation with tea. Every year, when tea picking time came, they would send the newly picked leaves to their relatives or friends living far away, showing that they missed them. When men of letters gathered for a party, tea and wine were the best accompaniment for poems and couplets, tea being particularly esteemed. In the latter half of Tang Dynasty, men of letters emulated monks to hold tea parties. Also in Tang Dynasty, Purple Bamboo Shoot Tea and Sun Admiring Tea produced from Mount Guzhu were tribute tea, known far and near. In the time of tea selection every spring, local officials supervised in person, and held an annual tea party where scholars and celebrities assembled. This was a much-told story then. Tea party got even more popular in Song Dynasty, spreading all over the country. Congenial scholars took turns to hold tea parties. He who provided low-quality tea or cooked tea badly would be punished.

Tea is the object of past scholars' praise and description. In all ages there are numerous poems, paintings, and calligraphic works about tea. For scholars, tea is noble and leaves much room for reflection, embodying high morality. A dialogue between Su Shi and Sima Guang in Song Dynasty well demonstrated this. Sima Guang asked Su Shi, "Tea and Chinese ink are quite opposite in nature because tea needs to be white while Chinese ink needs to be black, tea tends to be strong while Chinese ink tends to be light, and tea is better new while Chinese ink is better old. How come you like them both so much?" Su Shi answered the question very

cleverly.

"Tea and ink have things in common, too. Rare tea and good ink both emit nice smell and both have hard shell, so they are quite similar in virtue. They are like two men of honor. In appearance one is black and ugly while the other is white and beautiful, but they are actually equally lofty at heart." What Su Shi said was approved of by Sima Guang.

A part of tea utensils made from bamboo to hold tea food. Provided by Huang Rui.

Tea embodies the moral ideal of Chinese scholars. For this reason, tea as a gift has become an important way of nurturing friendship and sentiment between them. Ouyang Xiu of Song Dynasty had spent 18 years writing a book. He cherished it very much and especially asked the calligrapher Cai Xiang to write the prefatory stone inscription for him. In return for the favor, Ouyang Xiu gave Cai Xiang the most valuable Huishan well water and Dragon & Phoenix Cake, which greatly pleased Cai Xiang, for he thought this gift was "refined and unconventional."

Not only friends and acquaintances used tea to improve relationship, even strangers became best friends for their mutual fondness of tea. The famous essayist Zhang Dai (1597–1679) wrote such a story. He often heard from friends that an old man whose surname was Min was very good at cooking tea, so he went to visit him. Seeing Zhang Dai, old man Min suddenly remembered that he had forgot his walking stick, so he hurried back while Zhang Dai waited patiently. Returning with his walking stick, the old man was fairly surprised to see Zhang Dai still there. Zhang Dai told the old man his purpose and refused to leave until he drank a cup of tea cooked by him. Pleased with this, old man Min invited Zhang Dai to a special tea room and got the tea ready very

< Elegant tea utensils can add some romantic sense to tea-tasting. Provided by Huang Rui.

'Tea Art'
The Song period saw the rise of a kind of legerdemain of the tea world which was called at the time 'Tea Art'. Those who had mastered this skill could with one stir of a teaspoon produce on the surface of the tea all kinds of pictures, and this was seen as a kind of divination. The most skilful practitioners could even conjure up the traces of a poetic text, which was close to witchcraft. We can see from this what heights of skill were attained in things to do with tea by the people of the Song dynasty.

soon. Already a master of tea, Zhang Dai accurately told the history of the apparatus, the leaves and the water. Old man Min was so rejoiced to meet a man so proficient in tea for the first time in 70 years that they two sympathized with each other and became close friends since then.

People like Zhang Dai—loving tea, understanding tea, and enjoying tea—are not few. One of them is the great poet Bai Juyi (772–846), who is perhaps the most mass-friendly poet in old China. Every time he finished a poem, he would read it to an old lady. If she didn't understand it, he would modify the poem until she did. Bai's poems were highly popular among the contemporaries. Even geishas prided themselves on being able to sing his *Ode on Lute*. Bai Juyi was addicted to tea, often took tea with local monks during his tenure in Hangzhou and delighted therein. He had written over 20 poems on tea and even wrote biography for tea, comparing it to a noble and capable minister. Many people copied Bai's poems to trade for tea in the market. For Bai, who was devoted to tea his whole life, this must have been a big comfort.

Li Qingzhao (1084–c.1151) of Song Dynasty is a most eminent female poet in Chinese history. She also stands for the tea-loving females. Li and her husband had a lot in common, both loving reading and tea. Li was very knowledgeable and could trace the origin of a quotation to the exact row of an exact page in an exact book. She often betted with her husband and the winner got to drink tea first. Li Qingzhao won the bet more often and would laugh heartily with a tea cup in hand. But the tea often spilled out because of her laughing and she ended up drinking none. Later, Song Dynasty was threatened by ethnic groups and lost the territory in the north of Yangtze River. Li Qingzhao's husband was killed in the wartime chaos. Losing both a family and a country, Li's poems were filled with sadness and bitterness. The once pastoral life of tea, poem, and music could only come back in memory.

Enjoy Tea-time

The word Teahouse stemmed from Ming Dynasty and became common after Qing Dynasty. Except for that, there are also other names like tea building, tea mill, tea shop, tea garden, tea room, etc. It is a special location for people to drink tea, relax and have fun. It is also an epitome of two kinds of tea cultures of China, one upscale and the other folksy

The predecessor of teahouse is tea stand. A myth novel has it that an old lady in Western Jin (265–316) sold tea in the market every day. Buyers came and went nonstop from dawn to dusk, but the lady's tea never decreased. Teahouse in its real sense was born in Tang Dynasty and blossomed in Song Dynasty and continued developing in Ming and Qing dynasties. This developing journey of teahouse is quite similar to that of tea itself. After 1960's, teahouse almost disappeared. It met its renaissance only till the reform and opening up policy of 1978. Now in many cities of China teahouse runs neck and neck with cafes. It is an appealing place for the young and indicates a fashionable lifestyle.

During its long history of development, Chinese tea culture develops different characteristics and contains two sides of connotations—the upscale and the folksy. For the upscale side, men of letters or several close friends got together. They either cooked tea near

The Surroundings for Drinking Tea

From the Song dynasty on, tea drinking was regarded by people of official and literati status as a kind of refined spiritual enjoyment, and so they were very particular about the surroundings in which they drank their tea. Tranquillity was the guiding principle, and they required such things as buildings with a terrace, a quiet room, and well lit windows, perhaps in a Buddhist or Daoist monastery, where they could listen to the wind blowing in the pine trees, or gaze at winding streams or the moon seen through bamboos. There as they drank their tea they might sit in quiet meditation, or recite or compose poetry, or engage in refined conversation, or read. Of course there were plenty of people who liked to drink tea alone, but it was still more satisfying to be able to share one's joys with two or three companions who really appreciated tea. So even today, the tea houses in cities still favour an atmosphere of quiet seclusion. In their décor they aim at an old-style cultivated simplicity, and in many cases they use incense and classical Chinese music to create a suitable atmosphere for drinking tea.

a lovely well or on a rock, or tasted tea in a dense forest or among straight bamboos, reciting poems and verses at the same time. As to the folksy side, tea held a different meaning for common plebeians. Men of letters thought sip was the essence of tea drinking while large gulp spoiled the charm of it. However, for the plebeians tea was the best thirst reliever. The "Big Bowl Tea" in Beijing in late Ming Dynasty was a good example of the folksy culture of tea drinking. The tea stand consisted of only a table and several stools, very simple. The bowls were made of crude porcelain and leaves were cheap too. Workers after a hard day or travelers after a long trip took a rest at the stand. They would finish a big bowl of tea in one mouthful and then wiped away the tea drops in mouth end with the back of their hands. In comparison to scholars' leisurely tasting and little sips, this had its own appeal of generosity and heroism. The history of teahouse can best display the collision, merging, integration and division of the two kinds of tea culture in China.

A corner of an elegant tea house. Photo by Li Yuxiang.

Song Dynasty was the golden time for Chinese tea culture, when teahouse existed everywhere in city and even carried its way to village, almost the same quantity as restaurants. To beat others, every teahouse beat its brains to attract customers. First, it put great efforts in decoration. Teahouses of Song Dynasty were almost all decorated golden, lacquered, elegant and tidy, with flowers and calligraphic works or paintings of celebrities within. Some teahouses set up shelves to put rare plants to draw customers' attention. After Qing Dynasty, with the introduction of western culture, teahouses took on some new features as well. Some luxurious western-styled teahouse also came into being. Some teahouses were situated

< The people who like tea have less or more a peaceful and tranquil mood when tasting tea. Provided by Huang Rui.

in picturesque suburb, under a melon pavilion or bean shed, in a grape garden or near a pool. So they could meet customers' needs in different seasons. Customers could take a walk in the countryside in spring, avoid the heat in summer, watch maple leaves in autumn, and appreciate snow and plum blossoms in winter. Because of their special function, these teahouses were

The tea houses stressing cultural atmosphere. Photo by Li Yuxiang.

much welcomed. In order to gain a larger market, many teahouses even used carts and shoulder poles to take tea to the market at night. Sellers had to cry out loudly and even put flowers on head to appeal customers. Some other teahouses also functioned as hotels and bathrooms.

The primary function of teahouse was for tea drinking, so it went to great lengths to better itself in this aspect, inventing new varieties all the time. In winter, teahouse owners added cold-resisting tonics in tea. In summer, they added heat-dispelling medicines and sold sweetened bean paste, coconut wine, bittern plum water, pawpaw juice, and other beverages. The choice of tea apparatus was more and more particular too. New varieties invented by various teahouses were kept in exquisite porcelain

< The tea house with the style of combining Chinese and western cultures. Photo by Li Yuxiang.

bottles, set on red-lacquer plates, and placed in the most eye-catching spot in the teahouse, becoming a second signboard. Some teahouses used little pretty tin pot, red-clay oven and charcoal fire to stew rain water, and cooked West Lake Longjing and other fame tea. Teahouses also employed professionals to take charge of cooking tea, who were called "tea doctor."

To gain customers, teahouses usually introduced some entertainments. Some teahouses hired geishas and musical band to play music or sing songs; some acted as a school and taught music fans how to play and sing; some provided chess, Chinese chess, and conundrums, functioning like an arena of intelligence. The most common was to hire storytellers to tell historical anecdotes, myths and legends, and love stories between a bright boy and a beautiful girl. Storytellers were very eloquent and their stories were vivid and real, full of humor and wit. One story could last two or three months. Storytellers always stopped at the key moment so that the audience would come the next day to follow the story. In this way many people became big fans of the storyteller and regular customers in the teahouse as well. Story listening and tea drinking had separate bills. The storyteller borrowed the teahouse's place and teahouse sold more tea because of the story, so it was a two-win situation. Audience paid storyteller for the story and storyteller paid 30% of his income to the teahouse owner. This form of tea plus story exerted big influence on Chinese literature. Early novels about knights originated from these teahouse stories. But novelists transformed oral language into written language, with some modification and rearrangement.

Teahouse also played an indelible role for opera.

Tea House is an important place for leisure in modern city. Photo by Li Yuxiang.

< The host's interest of a tea house can often influence guests'. Photo by Li Yuxiang.

Some even say that "opera is an art irrigated by tea juice." Teahouse was not only a place for storyteller to show his talent, but also a stage for opera performance. At the end of 19th century, Zha Family Teahouse and Guanghe Teahouse of Beijing, Dan Gui Tea Garden and Tian Xian Tea Garden of Shanghai were well known locations for opera performance. Teahouse owner paid the troupe at first. Audience entered without tickets, only paying for the tea. Even theatres for opera alone often offered tea to audience. Some even were named as Teahouse. Opera had a special costume called "Tea Clothes," featured in blue blouse, big collar, and half length. This kind of clothes was first known as teahouse work garment, but later it became symbol of the whole working class. Most playwrights in the past loved drinking tea, of whom the famous playwright Tang Xianzu (1550–1616) of Ming Dynasty was a representative. He named his house "Jade Tea Hall" and the dramatic school he started was consequently called School of Jade Tea Hall. The spirit of tea has been rooted in opera. In south China, an opera is directly named after tea as "Tea Picking Opera," telling stories through songs and dances. This opera has its earliest embryo in the folksongs and dances performed in tea picking activities.

Teahouse plays an irreplaceable role in interpersonal communication. In ancient China, people sent tea in funeral as well as in wedding. But many people were often too busy to remember certain occasions and unintentionally offended others. With teahouse, this kind of situation was avoided. Teahouses introduced the service of "order and send" to solve this problem in particular. "Order and Send" means that customers entrusted teahouse to send certain tea to certain houses on special occasions to show good wish and blessing. This is similar to today's ordering flowers for people in florist shops.

Teahouse was not always noisy. Some "Simple Tea House" was featured in its simplicity and quietness. Some teahouses set special private rooms or sanctums to satisfy customers' different requirements. For this reason, businessmen and officials used to take teahouses as places for discussion or negotiation, and many trades and policies were decided this way. In some regions of Sichuan Province, there used to be a custom of "drink talking tea." In times of civil disputation on house, land or marriage, plebeians would not take the trouble to appeal to local authorities, but preferred to ask someone to mediate. This was called "drink talking tea." During that period, parties involved in the disputation invited prestigious and strong minded elders to mediate. Entering the teahouse, the parties first served tea to everyone present, and then stated the ins and outs of the affair and lodged their own claims. The involved parties finished, mediators (called arbitrator) sitting at the two tables near the door judged according to what they said. Generally speaking, once a decision was reached, disputing parties should unconditionally observe it. The losing party had to pay for the tea during the mediation as legal cost. "Drink talking tea" is a folk way of settling disputation. Yet once the mediation failed and disputation didn't get solved, there would be even more problems and disturbances. Therefore, at the end of Qing Dynasty and beginning of the Republic of China (early 20th century), many teahouses had notices like "Talking tea not allowed" posted, which was a peculiar phenomenon at a peculiar historical time just like "State-affair discussion banned."

The disappearance of teahouse in ancient China was the result of developed commodity economy. In Song Dynasty—the time of teahouse's prosperity, the population of capital Bianliang (today's Kaifeng of He'nan Province) reached 260,000 at one time. Afterwards, people of Nurchen nationality occupied Bianliang and Song had to transfer its capital to Lin'an (today's Hangzhou of Zhejiang Province). Lin'an was even bigger, with mongers and underlings in every avenue and alleyway and nonnative people several times more than native people. In such a big metropolis where the pace of life was so quick, a great many people didn't have time to cook, so they bought ready-made food in nearby

An old man drinking tea in a teahouse in Chengdu. Photo by Zhang Hongjiang.

A tea house with strong atmosphere of life in Sichuan. Photo by Chen Jin, Provided by *China Tourism*, Hong Kong.

shops. Teahouses supplied tea-accompanying snacks for customers, so if busy, many people just had some tea and snacks or ate tea-soaked rice in teahouses, just to temporarily alleviate hunger and thirst. Thus teahouses got a function of noshery, which could be considered the earliest form of Chinese fast food. When Qing Dynasty came and urbanization quickened its pace, teahouses also increased. In Beijing alone there were as many as over 30 famous teahouses, while there were above 800 in Hangzhou, big and small. In Shanghai, teahouses stood in numbers near the old Town God's Temple, forming a peculiar sight of tea market. People could bring tea to teahouses to cook and only had to pay for the water. The variety of tea-accompanying snacks was large, including local specialties like dried catsup, melon seeds, tiny plates of fruit, crisp cakes with sesame, spring roll, sugar-oil steamed bread, and so on.

Teahouse was a micro world where people of all walks gathered. In addition, teahouse didn't have a time limit, so the advantage of longtime sitting naturally made it the center of information collection and distribution. Tea doctor in a teahouse was the most informative man. Had one had anything to ask, he was the right guy to go to. A noblewoman in Song Dynasty lost her cat, so she had hundreds of pictures of the cat painted and posted in all major teahouses, like today's notice of "Lost" in newspaper. The tea-loving Chinese writer Laoshe wrote a famous play Teahouse. Based on the ups and downs of a teahouse, the play demonstrated a half-century social turbulence from 1898 to 1945, vividly depicting a picture of all kinds of people living in a troubled time. Teahouse is written in 1956. With less than 50,000 words, it covers rich social contents, covering more than 70 characters, 50 of whom have names or nicknames. These characters include figures of high positions, underdogs at the bottom of social ladder, boss and lads in teahouses, favored eunuchs, despicable pimps and scourings, entrepreneurs who believe in saving China through industry, old and new secret agents and hatchet men, storytellers, physiognomists, deserters, and kind-hearted workmen, embracing almost all levels of the society. Teahouse is divided into three scenes, each taking place at a different time. The play doesn't utilize massive historic scenes, but uses different characters' fortune to refract the vicissitude of the entire society. All activities are confined within the teahouse too, which, like a mirror, displays one by one the diverse human beings. In view of this, Laoshe took much pain to describe the teahouse, through which he delineated the peculiar teahouse culture of China. For instance, at that time people could buy snacks like "mixed meat noodle"; teahouse was not merely for tea drinking, either, but was a public place for intercommunication; customers could bring tea leaves themselves and frequenters could buy on credit; storyteller and teahouse were in an interdependent relation, and so forth.

Though teahouse reflects the two sides of tea culture, it more often than not appears as a representative of the folksy side. Though it was in high fashion for a period, it was still low and cheap in the eyes of scholars and bureaucrats. Moreover, the trend of pure tea advocated by scholars went against the general practice of teahouse's adding condiments in tea. After Ming Dynasty, with teahouse's getting more and more elegant, it was gradually accepted by scholars, and some well known tea experts resorted there. A lot of senior officials liked going to teahouse, and the idle youngsters of the Eight Banners (an establishment of army in early Qing Dynasty) took teahouse as the best place for killing time. Emperor Qianlong built a royal teahouse—"Mutual Joy Garden" —in the Garden of Perfection and Light, meaning to enjoy with all civilians. In times of New Year, Mutual Joy Garden opened trade streets which resembled commercial streets of common people, with shops, restaurants, teahouses and the like on each side. Even the peddling shout was imitated quite true to life. The regal family of Qing Dynasty enjoyed folk fun here, and in this way teahouse climbed its way from public streets to palaces.

Walking in street in China today, you will find all kinds of teahouse everywhere. They either take the form of south China gardens with bridge and pool, kiosk and pavilion, meandering path and flowers, and arch and corridor, or they imitate country taverns to pursue pastoral rustic charm, or take up a modern style designed and decorated to be vigorous and fashionable. Teahouse today has become a symbol of taste and is considered as part of fashion. Entering these teahouses, you can hear melodious and relaxing music and smell distant tea fragrance. Teahouse provides chess, poker, and other entertainments. You can also order snacks or fast food when hungry. Teahouse continues to play an important role in the life of Chinese people. Nowadays Chinese teahouse is often called "Tea Art House" where ladies perform different styles of Chinese tea ceremony for customers, so teahouse serves to revive the traditional culture of China.

Appendix:
Chronological Table of the Chinese Dynasties

The Paleolithic Period	Approx. 1,700,000–10,000 years ago
The Neolithic Age	Approx. 10,000–4,000 years ago
Xia Dynasty	2070–1600 BC
Shang Dynasty	1600–1046 BC
Western Zhou Dynasty	1046–771 BC
Spring and Autumn Period	770–476 BC
Warring States Period	475–221 BC
Qin Dynasty	221–206 BC
Western Han Dynasty	206 BC–AD 25
Eastern Han Dynasty	25–220
Three Kingdoms	220–280
Western Jin Dynasty	265–317
Eastern Jin Dynasty	317–420
Northern and Southern Dynasties	420–589
Sui Dynasty	581–618
Tang Dynasty	618–907
Five Dynasties	907–960
Northern Song Dynasty	960–1127
Southern Song Dynasty	1127–1279
Yuan Dynasty	1206–1368
Ming Dynasty	1368–1644
Qing Dynasty	1616–1911
Republic of China	1912–1949
People's Republic of China	Founded in 1949